HISTORIC PAPERS ON THE CAUSES OF THE CIVIL WAR

by

Eugenia Dunlap Potts

of the Lexington, Ky. Chapter of the U.D.C.

and

Mildred Lewis Rutherford

Historian General of the U.D.C. 1911-1916

THE CONFEDERATE
REPRINT COMPANY
☆　☆　☆　☆
WWW.CONFEDERATEREPRINT.COM

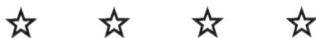

Historic Papers on the Causes of the Civil War
by Eugenia Dunlap Potts
and Mildred Lewis Rutherford

Originally Published in 1909
by Ashland Printing Company
Lexington, Kentucky

Originally Published in 1916
by The Mildred Rutherford Historical Circle
Birmingham, Alabama

Reprint Edition © 2016
The Confederate Reprint Company
Post Office Box 2027
Toccoa, Georgia 30577
www.confederatereprint.com

Cover and Interior Design by
Magnolia Graphic Design
www.magnoliagrapicdesign.com

ISBN-13: 978-0692646748
ISBN-10: 0692646744

CONTENTS

☆ ☆ ☆ ☆

CHAPTER ONE
The Old South
by Eugenia Dunlap Potts
[Read Before the Lexington Chapter U.D.C., February 14, 1909]

☆ ☆ ☆ ☆

No pen or brush can picture life in the old Southern States in the ante-bellum days. The period comprehends two hundred and fifty years of history without a parallel. A separate and distinct civilization was there represented, the like of which can never be reproduced. Socially, intellectually, politically and religiously, she stood pre-eminent, among nations. It was the spirit of the Cavalier that created and sustained our greatness. Give the Puritan his due, and still the fact remains. The impetus that led to freedom from Great Britain, came from the South. A Southern General led the ragged Continentals on to victory. Southern jurists and Southern statesmanship guided the councils of wisdom. The genius of war pervaded her people. She gave presidents, cabinet officers, commanders, tacticians and strategists. Her legislation extended the country's territory from the Atlantic to the Pacific.

A writer aptly says:

For more than fifty formative years of our history the Old South was the dominating power in the nation, as it had been in the foundation of the colonies out of which came the Republic, and later in fighting its battles of independence and in forming its policies of government. * * * Whatever of strength or symmetry the republic had acquired at home, or reputation it had achieved abroad, in those earlier crucial days of its history, was largely due to the patriotism and ability of Southern statesmanship. Why that scepter of leadership has passed from its keeping, or why the New South is no longer at the front of national leadership, is a question that might well give pause to one who recalls the brave days when the Old South sat at the head of the table and directed the affairs of the nation.

There was the manor and there was the cabin. Each head of the house was a potentate in his own domain – an absolute ruler of a principality as marked as in feudal times, without the despotism of the feudal system.

The plantation of the old regime was tastefully laid out for beauty and productiveness. Flower gardens and kitchen gardens stretched away into the magnificence of orange trees, shady avenues and fruitful plants. Unbroken retreats of myrtle and laurel and tropical foliage, bantered the sun to do his worst. Flowers perfumed the air; magnolia bloom and other rich tree flora regaled the senses; extensive orchards yielded fruit of all kinds adapted to the soil and climate; vineyards were heavy with much bearing. Fields were carefully cultivated, till such a thing as the failure of crops was almost unknown. It was largely supplied with sheep and their wool, with geese, ducks, turkeys, guinea fowls, and every variety of poultry without stint. Eggs were gathered by the bushel, myriads of birds clouded the sun, and daily intoxicated their little brains with the juice of the black cherry. Herds of cattle were luxuriously pastured by Pompey and his sable mates. There were quantities of rich cheese, fresh butter, milk and cream. Vast barns were gorged with corn, rice and hay; hives were bursting with honey; vegetables were luscious and exhaustless; melons sprinkled and dotted many acres of patches; shrimp and fish filled the waters; crawfish wriggled in the ditches; raccoons and opossums formed the theme of many a negro ditty. Carriages and horses filled the stables, and splendid mules were well-fed and curried at the barns. High up on the cypress trees hung the grey moss with which the upholsterer at yon market place replenished his furniture vans. The farm produce alone yielded six or seven thousands a year, while the plantation crops of cotton, sugar, and rice were clear profit. Rows of white cabins were the homes of the colored citizens of the community. An infirmary stood apart for the sick. The old grandams cared for the children. Up yonder at the mansion house Black Mammy held sway in the nursery; Aunt Dinah was the cook; Aunt Rachel carried the housekeeper's keys; while Jane and Ann, the mulatto ladies' maids, flitted about on duty, and Jim and Jack "'tended on young marster and de gemman." Such hospitality as was made possible by that style of living can never repeat itself in changed conditions. Grant that these conditions are improved. Grant that the lifted incubus of slavery has opened the doors for the march of intellectual and industrial progress; the fact remains that the highest order of social enjoyment, and of the exercise of the charming amenities of life, was blotted out when the old plantation of Dixie land was divided up by the spoils of war.

It is interesting to read of the first attempt at a sugar crop in Louisiana by a Frenchman named Bore in 1794. His indigo plant, once so profitable, had been attacked and destroyed by a worm, and dire poverty threatened. He conceived the project of planting sugar cane. The great question was would the syrup granulate; and hundreds gathered to watch the experiment. It did granulate, and the first product sold for twelve thousand dollars – a large sum at that time.

The maker of the cotton gin worked another revolution in commerce, and rice proved to be an unfailing staple. Armies of negroes tilled the soil, and were happy in their circumscribed sphere, humanely cared for by the whites.

Enter the home and lo! a palace greets you. Massive mahogany furniture, now, alas! in scattered remnants, meets the eye at every turn. Treasures and elegant trifles of many lands attest the artistic taste of the owners. Gorgeous china, plate and glass are there in everyday use. Fruits of the loom in rarest silk and linen, embellish the chambers and luxury sits enthroned. The chatelaine, gracious and cultured, is to the manner born: and from season to season she fills her house with congenial people who are invited to come, but not, as with present house parties, told when to go. As long as they found it comfortable and convenient the latchstring was out. A guest was never permitted to pay for anything; expressage, laundry and all incidentals were as free as air. The question of money, nowadays impertinently thrust forth, was never hinted at in the olden time. It was considered bad form, and the luckless boaster of "how poor he was" would have been properly stared at as a boor as well as a bore.

For pastimes men had fishing and hunting, and for

women there were lawn games and indoor diversions. Speaking of the women of the South a writer aptly said: "They dwell in a land goodly and pleasant to the eye; a land of fine resources, both agricultural and mineral; where may be found fertile cotton fields, vast rice tracts, large sugar plantations, bright skies and balmy breezes. The whole land is plowed by mighty rivers, is ribbed by long mountain chains, and washed by the sea."

Fitting environment, we add, for the gorgeous residences, notably in Georgia and South Carolina, built by the nobility and gentry of the republic, and inherited by the descendants of the old colonial aristocracy. What wonder, that they held themselves aloof from the manual laborer, black or white, and that they were uncontaminated by the attrition of commercial competition. In the summer the family sought the cooler climate of old Kentucky or Virginia, or farther north to Saratoga, Long Branch, or some one of the then attractive resorts. They travelled in state, frequently bringing the family coach, and never without a retinue of servants. What a sensation they made! And money flowed like water. The young men, rich and idle, paid court to pretty girls, sure of a welcome from both parents and daughters, for to marry a Southern planter was to achieve a social victory for all time to come. The mechanical and athletic age had not yet dawned. The accepted escort must be a professional man, or else lord of a domain such as I have described. Pride and prejudice blinded judgment, and the aristocracy of merit alone was unappreciated.

And yet the Southern woman, even of great wealth, could not afford to be idle. She was not, save in exceptional cases, the useless, half-educated, irresponsible creature she has been represented. Some there are always and everywhere whose lives are given over to fads, fancies and frivolities. But the true mothers were priestesses at the home altar, and kept the sacred fires bright and burning. Their duty was to keep others busy, and to direct and oversee the vast domestic machinery of the home.

Their views were somewhat narrow, for as yet the bright sun of woman's emancipation was barely peeping over the horizon. Their minds did not grasp the vexed questions of theology, politics, or economics. They accepted the faith of their fathers, and shifted all burdens to stronger shoulders. They were eminently religious and charitable. Ways and means were at hand, and they did not bother their brains with isms and ologies. Regular attendance upon the nearest church, and reverence for the clergy, were prominent in their creed.

Education for the masses was not provided, as it is now; but the majority of the better class were finely educated, either at Northern schools, or by the governess, and tutor at home. In many cases where the wife was widowed, she nobly and intelligently arose to the management of business affairs. If misfortune came, and the woman felt obliged to earn a livelihood, it did not occur to her to seek it behind a counter or in a workshop as we do in this generation. She was inclined to walk in the old paths, and follow old customs. They believed their own skies were bluest, their own cornfields greenest, their tobacco finest, their cotton the whitest on earth. They were devoted to old friends, to old manners and customs, and gloried in their birthright.

In the line of literary productions the South was backward. Augusta Evans Wilson's remarkable novels, *Beulah*, *St. Elmo*, and others, were read and re-read, not for any lasting good, but for passing interest, and largely

for the glamour that invested a Southern writer. Madame
Le Vert produced *Souvenirs of Travel*, among the very
earliest of books on European scenes. Marion Harland's
works were read, and possessed the selling quality notwithstanding the bitter taste left by her humiliated hero-
ines. Caroline Lee Hentz, Mrs. Holmes, Mrs. South-
worth, and a small army of essayists in the field, clamored
for recognition; but time was when to see the Southern
woman in print was an innovation displeasing to the
household gods. Time came when the slumbering faculties were stirred into splendid and successful activity. The
depth of the natures hitherto unsounded arose to the new
demands right valiantly. We behold its fruits in the rearing
of splendid monuments, the erection of noble charity institutions, the endowing of colleges, the equipment of
missionaries, the awakening of wide philanthropies, and
in the higher lines of Christian endeavor. The men who
shouldered arms, from father to son, to defend their
States rights, were the same who, in times of peace, knew
no burdens of life save those they voluntarily assumed.
The women who sewed night and day upon garments for
field and hospital, were the same who were wont to em-
ploy their white hands with fragile china and heirloom
plate, or dally with needlework in the morning room.
These were the mothers who, standing by the slaughtered
first-born, gave his sword to the next son, and bade him
go at his country's call. There was the spirit of heroism
not surpassed by the heroes of the sterner sex. They suffered privations and terrors without a murmur.

   To visit one of these ante-bellum homes was a
privilege indeed. And something of the spirit of the ca-
naille of the French revolution must have animated the
foreign hordes, who, not content with confiscating these

captured palaces, ruthlessly cut and destroyed the richness and elegance they were beholding for the first time in their commonplace lives. It was not the spirit of conquest, but of vandalism, that animated them. Wanton destruction and not spoliation, common in war tactics, was their watchword. A domain fairer than Elysium opened to their astonished gaze, whenever they penetrated some sylvan grove where stood the plantation manor house.

Alas! for the old plantation days! Alas! for the easygoing spirit that marked the times! The long, pitiless, hot sun-days were not inspirers of extraordinary energy. Yankee thrift was as pigmy play to these owners of bursting coffers. The hurry and bustle of our Northern neighbors was an unknown quantity in their economy. It is to the forcible wresting from the South of their inherited institutions, of the machinery which made their social order possible, that the land of Dixie owes the prosperity and thrift of to-day. Evil was done and good came therefrom. Years of wasted substance and enforced poverty were groped through, till at last the day-star rose upon new industries. Hands and feet and awakened faculties spring to the keynote of progress, and "Our days are marching on."

[Here were inserted in the manuscript twenty pages from the diary of the Historian, written when, as a school girl, she visited with her parents some of the sugar plantations of Louisiana. They give the picture by an eyewitness of the social and commercial life in the South; but while, perhaps, interesting in the reading of a paper, are not necessary, in print, to the theme.]

Future generations may hug to themselves the consolation that we were pulled down only to be built up again in greater prosperity, under a different order of things.

The tears and woes of the old South may change into smiles and good cheer, forgetting the glory that once encircled us like a radiant halo. But many there are who feel that "Such things were, and were most dear to us!" These look back with brimming eyes, and force down the rising sob, as they sorrowfully murmur, "My native land, good night."

CHAPTER TWO:
Slavery
by Eugenia Dunlap Potts
[Read March 14, 1909.]

☆　☆　☆　☆

In my first paper I endeavored to present a picture of the sunny Southland in the ante-bellum days, when wealth and culture and hospitality were the watchwords of the hour – before the invasion of hostile hordes had vandalized the sacred old traditions, and crumbled the household gods in the dust.

But long before the tocsin of civil war had sounded there were mutterings of thunder in the halls of Congress, and the cloud, at first no bigger than a man's hand, was yearly gathering force, till it finally burst in a cyclone of passion and prejudice and tyranny, and swept all before it in one besom of destruction. That the question of slavery lay at the root of the dissension cannot be doubted by any who are conversant with the political history of the United States. The tariff rulings had their weight, as did the unfair division of new territory: but the main issue was negro slavery, which, always a stumbling-block to the North, had most violently agitated the whole country for eleven years before the appeal to arms.

Negro laborers were brought to Virginia and sold as slaves, fifty years after the first cargo landed at Jamestown. In the year 1619, a Dutch vessel brought over twenty negroes to be thus held in bondage. To the men who watched the landing of this handful of Africans it was doubtless an unimportant matter, yet it was the beginning of a system that had an immense influence upon our country. In those days few persons in the world opposed slavery. Even kings and queens made money out of the traffic. But for tobacco slavery would not have taken such a hold on America. When it was found that the negro made the cheapest laborer for cultivating the plantation many more were imported.

They were also employed in the New England and Middle States, largely as household servants, the soil not being favorable to the production of rice, indigo, cotton and sugar, which were the staples of Southern agriculture. Moreover, the African is not physically adapted to the northern climate. He was especially liable to tubercular disease – hence he was sold to the Southern planters, except in a few cases where the Puritan spirit caused his emancipation.

In the year that Harvard College was erected, 1636, the first slave ship built in America was launched at Marblehead, Mass. It brought a large cargo of slaves to be sold to the settlers. During the one hundred years preceding 1776, millions of slaves had been imported to the States. King George III favored the institution, and forbade any interference with the colonies in this matter. The horrors of slavery in Massachusetts, as recorded by reliable documents of the period, far exceed all that has been charged against the South, by *Uncle Tom's Cabin*, or any other records of fact or romance. *The Encyclopedia of Political Economy and United States History*, Vol. 3, page 733, has the following taken from the *New York Evening Post*:

> During the eighteen months of the years 1859-60 eighty-five slave ships (giving their names) belonging to New York merchants, brought in cargoes annually of between 30,000 and 60,000 African slaves, who were sold in Brazil, there being great demand for them in that country, owing to new industries. Old Peter Faneuil built Faneuil Hall with slave money, and many other fortunes were thus made.

Thomas Jefferson says in his autobiography that though the Northern people owned very few slaves themselves, at the time of the writing of the Declaration of Independence, yet they had been pretty considerable carriers of slaves to others. In 1761 Virginia and South Carolina, alarmed at the rapid increase of slaves, passed an act restricting their importation, but as many persons in England were growing rich from the trade the act was negatived, or vetoed. While providing in the Constitution of the United States for the Southern planters to hold slaves, the North thought that the laws that were in the course of events to be passed for prohibiting their foreign importation, would so work out so that the institution would die a natural death. They little dreamed that economical and political conditions were destined to fasten it upon the South. At the framing of the Constitution slaves were held in all the States except Massachusetts, and she had only very lately abolished the institution. The South owned twice as many, by reason of her special agricultural products, and even at this early day the slavery question became sectional. Mason's and Dixon's line, which was an imaginary boundary between

Pennsylvania and Maryland, was recognized as the division line between the free and slave States.

[Here are omitted several pages illustrating the utter absence of affinity between the two sections of the country, introduced in the manuscript as social, not historical, matter.]

During the Revolutionary war it was deemed expedient to enlist the colored race as soldiers. In Rhode Island they were made free by law, on condition that they enlisted in the army, and this measure met with Gen'l Washington's approval. After the Declaration of Independence, in 1777, Vermont, Pennsylvania and Massachusetts freed their slaves and permitted them to vote, "provided they had the requisite age, property and residence." The 15th Amendment of a later day was an outrageous document, framed regardless of any such qualifications, but giving the ignorant black man rights even above the white citizens.

In order to induce the Southern States to accept the Federal Constitution in the beginning and have the country become a Union of States, the opposers of slavery had to compromise the use of terms, and take measures that seemed expedient. They fondly hoped as time rolled on, to legislate the freedom of slaves. But the invention of the cotton gin by Eli Whitney, in 1793, immensely increased the value of slave labor, and forever fastened the institution upon the Southern planters, so far as future legislation was concerned. It had been so difficult to separate the cotton fiber by hand, requiring a whole day to one pound, that it was only a minor product; but now the wonderful source of revenue made possible by the new invention, caused the importation of many more slaves, and cotton growing in a million acres became king of the marts. The planter would not willingly give up his property honestly acquired, and plainly permitted by the Constitution.

Slavery was a constant obstacle to the perfect Union of States. In 1790 during the second session of the first Congress, the Quakers and the Pennsylvania Abolition Society, through Benjamin Franklin, its President, prayed Congress to restore to liberty those held in bondage. The question was debated in the House in a warm, excited manner. Members from South Carolina and Georgia argued that slavery, being commended by the Bible, could not be wrong; that the Southern States would not have entered into the Confederacy unless their property had been guaranteed them, and any action of the general Government looking to the emancipation of slavery would not be submitted to. They said that South Carolina and Georgia could only be cultivated by negro slaves, for the climate, the nature of the soil, and ancient habits, precluded the whites from performing the labor. If the negro were freed he would not remain in those States; hence all the fertile rice and indigo swamps must be deserted and would become a wilderness. Furthermore the prohibiting of the slave trade was at that time unconstitutional. James Madison poured oil on the troubled waters by stating that Congress could not interfere according to constitutional restrictions, "Yet," he said, "there are a variety of ways by which it could countenance the abolition; and regulations might be made to introduce the freed slaves into the new States to be formed out of the Western territory." (In parenthesis I remark that if Madison could have looked down the years, he would have found that even though emancipated, the negro will not leave the white settlements. Take our own little city of Lexington where some 17,000 of them are congregated, living in discomfort and poverty in most cases; yet their nature is to depend in some fashion upon their white neighbors and employers.)

It was finally decided in the House that Congress could not prohibit the slave trade until the year 1808 – that Congress had no authority to interfere in the emancipation of slaves, or in the treatment of them within any of the States. This last resolution which is of great historic importance, may be found on page 1523 of the II Vol. of *Annals of Congress.*

Washington wrote to David Stuart in June 1790: "The introduction of the Quaker memorial respecting slavery was, to be sure, not only ill-timed, but occasioned a great waste of time."

In 1793 the Fugitive Slave law was passed, whereby a runaway slave captured in a free State, must be returned to his owner. As the new States were admitted into the Union they came in for the most part alternately free and slave States. This was done to preserve the balance of power in Congress.

The great aggressive Abolition movement that led eventually to the Civil War, had its birth in 1831. Fanatics like John Brown, and Mrs. Harriet Beecher Stowe, fanned into flame the sparks that had so long-smouldered, till the helpless negro was dragged from his havens of peace and comfort. If he felt bitterness towards the whites, what was to prevent his rising in insurrection and slaying them all? There were plantations where 600 or 700 slaves were governed by two or three white owners. They occupied little villages and had no care upon earth. They had their pastimes and religious worships. "The courtly old planter, high bred and gentle, the plantation 'uncle' who copied the master's manners; and the broad-bosomed black mammy, with vari-colored turban, spotless apron, and beaming face, the friend and helper of every living thing in cabin or mansion, formed a trio we love to remember." The black woman cared more for her white nursling than her own child. This seems unnatural, but it was true; and many of us recall the times that the mistress of the house had to interfere to prevent the kitchen mother from cruelly whipping her naughty offspring. Some relic of ancient African barbarism still lingered in their untutored minds. We loved our colored playmates, and their sable mothers and fathers. Many a winning story of "way down upon de ole plantation" has been truthfully told. Will S. Hays has immortalized it in song.

A Southern writer has thus portrayed the Christmas time:

For weeks beforehand everything was full of stir and preparation. Holly and mistletoe and cedar were being put about the rooms of the big house to welcome home the boys and girls from school. Secret councils were held as to the Christmas gifts to be given to everyone, white and black. The woodpile was loaded with oak and hickory logs to make bright and warm the Christmas nights. The negro seamstresses were busy making new suits for all the servants.

The king was in the parlor counting out his money – to pay out for gifts of the season – and the queen was in the kitchen dealing bread and honey – to paraphrase Mother Goose. Into the stately plantation home, with its lofty white columns, its big rooms, and its great fireplaces, poured the sons and daughters, grandchildren, uncles and aunts, nephews and nieces. Assembled around the groaning board, the patriarch asked the divine blessing and the twin spirits of Christianity were rife in the land. There was only a fitful sleep for the small boys and girls, who were up at peep of day, stealing: from room to room crying "Christmas Gift!" Out on the back porches waited the negroes in grinning rows to follow the example. All week the cabin fires burned brightly and constant was the rejoicing over their treasures, not forgetting the grand eatables and the big bowl of egg-nogg.

Negroes are a religious as well as a superstitious race. At midnight Saturday it was their custom to ring the great plantation bell, and spend the next several hours in exhorting, praying and singing their curious, doleful hymns. The whites gave them instruction and training along these lines. Heart and conscience were alike cultivated – not alone the sounding brass and tinkling cymbal. Statistics show that there were 466,000 slaves belonging to churches in the South: Methodist, Baptist, Presbyterian, Episcopalian, and other sects. So the owners of these Christianized people thought that they were doing missionary work in saving them from the cannibalism of heathen Africa. Both men and women were taught trades and useful occupations. There were tanners, shoemakers, blacksmiths, farmers, gardeners, horticulturists and carpenters among the men. The women could sew, cook, card, spin, weave, knit, wash, iron, in fact what they produced in this way would put to shame the acquirements and accomplishments of free labor. Many of the older negroes refused to be freed, when the mighty proclamation came. They would not withdraw from the protection of "Old Marster." Look at the product of these two generations of freedom. What is he? Well we know the painful answer.

But while the buying of slaves for domestic, or

field service, was legitimate, the man who pursued the traffic as a business, and purchased merely to sell again, was despised. He was termed a "nigger-buyer," and was a pariah in the lowest sense of ostracism. It was claimed that there was a distinction with a very great difference. Three or four servants for ordinary household duties were deemed sufficient. On a farm more hands were needed, and the plantations further South required several hundred. The refractory slave of Kentucky and the border States, was sold "down the river" in commercial parlance, where the discipline of the rice, sugar, and cotton plantations kept in check his evil inclinations. There might have been cases of cruel punishment, but the rule was kindness – if for no other reason, the master would not injure that which stood for money, for property. The expense of keeping slaves was enormous. Where is the laborer of to-day who is furnished his house, clothing, doctors, medicine, and not a little pocket money on occasions?

The South employed her laborers to produce the great staple of cotton, which was to clothe mankind. They were properly clothed, fed and made comfortable. In addition, they were cared for when sick, and there existed the warmest affection for the majority of them. The world can nowhere show human beings as care-free in bondage as were the negroes of the ante-bellum days. Judge the Southern owner by the rule and not the exception. As well judge a town by its halt, maimed, blind, diseased and lawless citizens, as the slave owners by occasional acts of oppression to be found on the plantations. But it was the "Down east" Yankee overseer who was cruel – not the master. It was the African in New England who was denied religious teaching, and even baptism. There was no sympathy there, to quote from a writer, for the poor creatures transplanted from their native sunny clime, dying by hundreds from disease on the bleak Northern shores. It was merely a question of profit and loss. They were sold to the South as fast as they could be shipped. Even when the great hue and cry for freedom led the Northern Senators to legislate for the cessation of foreign slavery in 1808, these great philanthropists rushed over some 5,000 slaves to sell to the South before the limited date could come around. Many prominent rich men of New England made their money by this traffic, then pulled a long face of condemnation for the Southern planter, whose money had been paid over to swell the Northern coffers.

It is worthy of note that the South never owned or sailed a slave ship.

In 1861 Mr. C.C. Clay, of Alabama, made a bitter speech in the United States Senate. Part of his arraignment was that not a decade had passed that the North had not persecuted the South on account of her slaves.

You denied us Christian communion because you could not endure slave-holding. You refused us permission to sojourn, or even pass through the North with our property. You refused us any share of the lands acquired mainly by our diplomacy and blood and treasure. You robbed us of our property and refused to restore it.

The speaker went minutely into the outrages perpetrated by the Abolition party. The list of oppressions had reach a crisis. Meanwhile the cotton and the cane went on in Dixie land, to the weird ditties and the quaint folk-lore of the happy-go-lucky race. So the outbreak of the war found the American slave in the height of his prosperity, unmindful of so-called wrongs, and utterly unfit for the boasted freedom that was thrust upon him. The cruel decree was carried out, and millions of helpless beings were turned adrift without rudder or compass, to bemoan the loss of the good old times when they were provided with the comforts of life they were nevermore to know. With the moral question of slavery this paper has nothing to do. Facts, and facts alone, dictate the record. But who has been, and who is now, the friend of the erstwhile slave? The Northerner or the Southerner? Says one: "We have freed you, but we don't want you." Says the other: "We did not free you, but we will take you and make you comfortable. We love your people – you, who have rocked us on your faithful breasts – who have interlarded our very speech with your dialect, and who were our playmates in the joyous days of youth. We have laid your hoary heads in honored graves, and will treasure your memory till the final hour when death shall make all men equal."

CHAPTER THREE
Secession
by Eugenia Dunlap Potts
[Read April 11, 1909]

☆　☆　☆　☆

We seem not to have been a happy family during our first one hundred years as a Union of States. We quarrelled frequently among ourselves, and like the dissatisfied children of the household there was oft-threatened disruption. If you do not treat me fairly I will leave home, said the stubborn Northern child, no less than the warmhearted Southern offspring. And they stood alike in the attitude of going out the door the moment the provocation became unbearable. The right of secession and the thought of secession was frequently in the mind all along the infant years of the Republic. But the word "Secession" did not become a familiar term until the early sixties. Then the greeting was "Hello! old Secesh!" or "Are you secesh?" One might have thought that this awful thing the South had done was heard of for the first time, and had birth alone in the brains of the fiery aristocrats who tore themselves away from their plebean cousins; whereas history shows, as I have said, that every State believed it had a right to secede from the general Government by the wording of our

Constitution, so when the pressure grew too close the terms, "Southern Rights," and "Secession," became the slogan of battle and sounded the tocsin of war.

Let us begin at the beginning and get at the actual situation. The thirteen original colonies were as follows: Virginia settled by the English, called the Cavaliers, in 1607, became a royal colony in 1624. Massachusetts, settled by the Puritans in 1620, became a royal colony in 1629; New York, called Amsterdam, settled by the Dutch in 1623, became a royal colony in 1688; the English were in New York in 1664. New Hampshire, settled by Puritans in 1729, became a royal colony in 1679; Maryland, settled by Catholics from England, in 1632, became a royal colony in 1691; Connecticut, settled by Dutch and English in 1633, became a royal colony in 1662; Rhode Island was settled in 1638, and never became a royal colony. She was excluded from the New England federation because she harbored all kinds of religions. She especially reserved to herself a State government alone, and a right to secede in any case. So this terrible crime of secession had birth in that pious, patriotic North that so bitterly condemned the States of Dixie Land for clamoring for a future right.

Delaware, settled by Swedes in 1638, became a separate colony, owned by William Penn, in 1703. North Carolina, settled by Virginians and Quakers in 1653, became a royal colony in 1729; New Jersey settled by the English in 1665, became a royal colony in 1702. Pennsylvania, settled by Germans, Dutch and Scotch-Irish in 1681, was given by King Charles II of England, to Wm. Penn in 1770. South Carolina, settled by French Huguenots and Germans in 1691, became a royal colony in 1729. Georgia, the last English colony, was settled by the English in 1732 and had her royal charter in 1762.

I have given the colonial dates in regular order of chronology. A more convenient division may be made thus: the New England colonies were Massachusetts, New Hampshire, Connecticut and Rhode Island, all belonging to England except Rhode Island. The middle colonies were New York, Delaware, New Jersey and Pennsylvania, two belonging to England, and two to Wm. Penn. The Southern colonies were Georgia, Maryland, North Carolina, South Carolina and Virginia, all belonging to England. Brought together by common cause were English, French, Germans, Dutch, Swedes, Quakers, Episcopalians, Catholics and all desired forms of religious worship. Wise legislation indeed was needed to harmonize these conflicting elements and dispositions merely on general principles. But when grave questions came then trouble began. What was to the commercial interest of one section seemed to militate against the prosperity of the other, and the glorious ending of the war for independence was soon clouded by the acts of Congress concerning the polity of the United States.

The African Slave Trade, begun by the North for purposes of profit, became a bone of contention till the year 1808, when the law was passed against the further importation of foreign slaves. Those already owned and employed must on no account be disturbed. They might increase and multiply *ad libitum* on their own plantations, but they were the legitimate property of their owners. Even when Abraham Lincoln signed the Emancipation Act, he said that he had not the right as President to do it, but that it must be done as a war measure. By depriving the Southern soldier of his laborers, the homes must go to waste and the strife most cease.

Politically each of the original colonies was independent, had its own assembly and its own governor. From the very first this idea of State sovereignty was inherent, and consequently it was granted. The royal colonies sent all legislative acts to England to be approved or vetoed by the king. It must have required patience to await the going and returning of the documents across the "vasty deep" in that day. These royal colonies so governed by the king were New York, New Hampshire, New Jersey, Virginia and Georgia. In the proprietary colonies, or those granted by royalty to individuals, the owner appointed the governor, but the king exercised the right of veto in Pennsylvania and Delaware, but not in Maryland. The charter colonies were Massachusetts, Connecticut and Rhode Island. These held charters from the king permitting a complete government by themselves. At this time black slaves were in all the States. Even after the New England States had grown rich by the selling of the negroes to the South, where the climate suited their natures, they kept up the traffic in white slaves who, too poor to pay their passage to the new land flowing with milk and honey, sold themselves, hoping to buy back their freedom in the perhaps near future.

When the Constitution of the United States was framed many compromises were made. The framers had to select words with extreme care lest some State might refuse to join the federation. A notable compromise, and the very first quarrel, was the one just quoted in reference to placing the limitation of the slave trade as far ahead as 1808. The next disagreement was about the war debt. This was called the Assumption. The general Government had contracted a debt of $54,000,000 and the States, about $25,000,000. This was in 1790. Alexander Hamilton proposed that the Government assume the whole debt. Hence the word "assumption." The South argued that each

State should pay its own debt; that if the general Government assumed the State debts it would be taking away the sovereign rights that had been guaranteed them, viz: the right to do as they pleased with what was their own, and that national legislation had nothing to do with the question. About this time they were looking about for a site upon which to build the national capital. Sectional spirit ran high. New England declared that *her States would secede* if the South succeeded in defeating assumption and in getting the capital, too. So a compromise was effected. The Assumption bill passed, and the South got the capital, after the seat of government was established at Philadelphia during ten years. In this year, too, many petitions to abolish slavery were forced upon Congress. After a heated debate the fiat went forth that Congress could not take action till 1808.

Next came the adding of ten amendments to the Constitution, all for the purpose of protecting State rights. Thomas Jefferson became the leader of the Republican party, afterwards known as Democrats, and not to be confounded with the Republican party of to-day. There was a most bitter wrangle over the wording of the Constitution, during which even President Washington received abuse. *Threats of breaking up the Union were heard on all sides.*

Then there was a quarrel over the National Bank question. The first one was established at Philadelphia in 1791, and the United States became a stockholder. The purpose was to furnish a safe currency, and one that would be uniform throughout the States.

In 1791 Vermont, a part of New York, was admitted, a free State. In 1792 Kentucky, cut off from Virginia, entered as a slave State, and in 1796 Tennessee, given up by North Carolina, came in as a slave State. Our government was involved in trouble with other countries in regard to territory, but this sketch has chiefly to do with our disputes as a family. While John Adams was President, the successor of Washington, the Alien and Sedition Laws created a stir in the country. The Federalists gave the President power to send out of the country all foreigners whom he considered dangerous to the peace and safety of the United States. They feared that these foreign citizens, by their free speech and writings might involve us in a war with Great Britain. This was the Alien Law. The Democrats contended that they had a right to bring over all the foreigners they pleased and make them citizens. The Sedition Law condemned to fine or imprisonment any writer of false, scandalous, or malicious statement against the Government, Congress, or the President. The Democrats urged that this law took away freedom of speech and liberty of the press. Virginia, by James Madison, and Kentucky, by Thomas Jefferson, passed resolutions which have become famous in political history. Each set of resolutions proclaimed the Union to be only a compact between the States. They declared the Alien and Sedition laws to be unconstitutional, null and void. Virginia actually strengthened her military forces, and made ready for secession as far back as this date, 1799. The laws were not passed.

In 1803 Ohio, the 17th State, was ceded by Virginia, and was admitted – the first State carved from the Northwest Territory, and employed free labor.

The purchase of Louisiana from Napoleon in 1803 caused much discussion and interest. It comprised a vast area equal to the whole United States. Exploring expeditions were sent out to find what the unknown territory was like. Whenever there was a question of an acquisition to the Union the slave question was also in agitation. We next hear of secession when the Embargo Act was passed. In

1807 Congress, in order to avoid the war with Great Britain which was fated to come five years later, enacted that no American vessel should leave the country for foreign ports. New England, where commerce was still the chief industry, suffered most. She threatened to secede, and both Massachusetts and Connecticut proclaimed the right to nullify the law. Two years later the act was repealed and again the Union was saved. Truly Uncle Sam had restive children who could not be driven, but who might at times be coaxed into a good humor.

Now came the quarrel between the State Banks and the National Bank. The National Bank charter expired in 1811 and Congress refusing to grant another, it had to go out of business. In 1812 Louisiana, a slave State, came in to make the eighteenth addition.

When war with England was declared in order to protect our commerce, again the *New England States wanted to secede.* Bells were tolled, business was suspended, flags were at half-mast, and the war was condemned in town meetings – from the press and the pulpit. They believed it would ruin rather than protect commerce. So they wanted to run away by themselves. When the Administration called for militia these States refused to obey.

The Hartford Convention, just after our successful war with Great Britain, proposed some amendments to the Constitution, and justified secession as a remedy for an uncongenial Union, but one that "should not be resorted to except when absolutely necessary." They confirmed the Virginia and Kentucky resolutions. The Democrats openly charged that the object of the convention was disunion. The Federalist party went to pieces. A new National Bank was established – in 1816 – to continue twenty years. In 1817

Indiana, the second State from the Northwest Territory, became a member of the Union, with free labor. She was the 19th State, and asked permission to hold slaves, but Congress prohibited slavery north of the Ohio river. The North had ere this freed or sold her slaves, but the institution was legalized in the Southern States. There were now nineteen States and five territories, viz: Mississippi, Michigan, Illinois, Missouri, and Alabama. Emigration poured into the West. Each section of the young republic watched its own prosperity with jealous interest. The Tariff question caused excited sectional feeling. A tax on foreign goods for the sake of revenue only had satisfied everybody; but a protective tariff was unpopular with the South. The North, having manufactories, was glad to protect her infant industries. The South had no manufactories – only agricultural products, and her representatives combatted the measure with zeal. This tariff bill has always caused opposition, and a glance at the daily doings at Washington shows that it is still a bone of contention.

Mississippi was admitted as a State in 1817 with slaves; Illinois in 1818, free; and Alabama, in 1819, slave, making twenty-two States, eleven free, and eleven slave States – an equal division. In 1819 Florida was bought from Spain.

The greatest quarrel came when Missouri was talked of as a State. The South wanted her left free to choose slave labor; the North feared that this would give the Southern legislators control of the Senate. There were numerous slaves in Missouri Territory, and she wanted to retain them as a State. So angry were the debaters, and so heated the feeling, that it was feared the country would go to pieces. This was as far back as 1819. Maine, cut off from Massachusetts, now wanted to come into the Union. As she would be a free labor State, the Southerners would not vote for her admission unless Missouri could have slaves; hence the Missouri Compromise Bill, of which we have all heard. Senator Jesse B. Thomas, of Illinois, proposed this compromise. The terms of it admitted Missouri with slaves, but prohibited slavery in any other portion of the Louisiana Purchase north of a certain specified latitude, which was the southern boundary of Missouri. This quelled the matter for many years, but most of us have seen the celebrated steel engraving, where Henry Clay stands speaking on this question, and pouring oil on the troubled waters. His powerful oratory so often saved the country from dissension that he was termed the Great Pacificator. The gifted triumver, Henry Clay from Kentucky, Daniel Webster from Massachusetts, and John C. Calhoun from South Carolina, had labored through years to reconcile the national vexed questions. All three died in the early fifties, and remembering the results of their mighty genius, there were many to say, ten years after that if they had lived there would have been no war, save perhaps another war of words in Congress. But their patriotic heads were laid low, and there were none to take their places. The two sources of dissension, slavery and the tariff, were always on hand to make a stormy session, so that a detailed history of the wrangling among the North, South and West would be a tedious transcription. What suited one section was adverse to the best interests of the others. The South abided strictly by the wording of the Constitution. The North was ever ready to put a liberal construction on its meaning, and naturally they took issue.

In 1824 the Tariff question became so untenable

that some of the Southern States rebelled outright, and protested through their legislatures against the measure as unconstitutional. Some favored secession; others advocated nullification, and this was what was done. They nullified the law and refused to stand by it. Clamor for State rights was heard on every side. But they did not take this step till they had waited two or three years for Congress to give relief by reducing the tariff. In 1832 the crisis came; nullification was pronounced by South Carolina, and she forbade the collection of tariff duties in her own State. She also declared that if the United States used force, she would withdraw from the Union and organize a separate government. Andrew Jackson, who was President, determined to enforce the tariff law in the State, and asked Congress for the power to use the army to sustain the law. Volunteers had offered in South Carolina, and the country stood aghast at the prospect of civil war. Here again Henry Clay's eloquence saved the day. He proposed the measure of gradually reducing the tariff through a period of ten years till it would provide only for the expenses of the Government. This removed the cause of trouble, so South Carolina rescinded her act of nullification.

The South had continually yielded up portions of her immense territory to the Union, and thus far there had been an equal balance of power in the legislative voting of the two sections. The annexation of Texas raised a stormy conflict. The South hoped for a division of this large tract into five slave States. The North, as usual, wished to obtain the lion's share. In 1835 Arkansas was admitted a slave State. In 1836 Michigan came in with free labor. After the Mexican War the retrospect showed that since the Declaration of Independence the North had possessed herself of nearly three-fourths of all the territory added to the original States. She fought the annexation of Texas because it would be slave-holding. In 1845 Florida was admitted with slave labor. In the same year Texas came in as a slave State. In 1846 Iowa came in with free labor; in 1848 Wisconsin, also free. When California applied for admission in 1850 there was such bitter antagonism that it was universally feared the Southern States would secede from the Union. Should she be a free State there would then be no other State to offset it with slaves. It was finally decided to leave the choice to California herself. Henry Clay was again at hand to effect a satisfactory compromise. In a former paper I have referred to the Fugitive Slave Law, whereby runaway slaves should be captured and sent back to their owners. But about a decade before the war, a great Abolition wave had begun to flood the country. Thurlow Weed, William Lloyd Garrison, Parson Brownlow, John Brown and Mrs. Stowe, by the power of tongue and pen and printing press, endeavored to stir up the North to the pitch of fanatical desperation, and the slaves to revolt against their masters. It was not for the sake of the Union. Perish the Union, if only the slaves were freed. Drive out the Southern States if they refused to abolish them. Their acts and their words were the extreme of anarchy and tyranny.

Jealousy had long formed a vindictive element in their breasts. And how could the two sections be wholly fraternal? They had come from, not only different stocks of population, but from different creeds in religion and politics. There could be no congeniality between the Puritan exiles who settled upon the cold, rugged and cheerless soil of New England, and the Cavaliers who sought the brighter climate of the South, and who, in their baronial halls, felt nothing in common with roundheads and regicides.

In 1859 the tragic raid of John Brown at Harper's Ferry – his execution – and the startling effects of the open outbreak against slavery put the Southern States on guard. When the next presidential election came on it was apparent from Mr. Lincoln's debates with Mr. Douglas, what the future policy of the Government would be. When he therefore, won the election, the South withdrew her representatives from Congress, and her States from the Union. Secession, so long threatened by both sections in turn, had come at last. Everything had been done on the floor of the House to harmonize the issues, but without avail.

On December 20, 1860 South Carolina passed the ordinance of secession. On January 9, 1861, Mississippi followed; Florida, January 10; Alabama, January 11; Georgia, January 19; Louisiana, January 26; Texas, February 1; Virginia, April 17; Arkansas, May 6; North Carolina, May 20; Tennessee, June 8.

To sum up the causes for the secession of the South:

1. The State had always been supreme: each was a distinct sovereignty, not subject to the general government in matters of their own home rule.

2. The interests of the South were injured by the burden of tax for the benefit of the North.

3. The Republican party had determined that slavery should not be admitted in the territories – the Republicans were in power, and foreseeing further interference in their rights, the South thought the time had come to form an independent government.

4. The North refused to accept the compromise

proposed by Senator John J. Crittenden of Kentucky, which might have averted the war. Nor would she consent to submit the matter to a vote of the people; hence there was no chance for harmony. The aggressive measures of the North were such as no self-respecting State in the South could endure.

It had come to be a habit in Congress, to insult the South because she held slaves.

Reason and right alike succumbed to prejudice and hatred, and the dissatisfied States, weary of wrong and oppression, sounded the note of separation; and from every throat burst the refrain:

> We are a band of brothers,
> Native to the soil,
> Fighting for the property,
> We've gained by honest toil.
> Hurrah! Hurrah! for Southern rights hurrah!
> Hurrah! for the Bonnie Blue Flag
> That bear a single star.

CHAPTER FOUR
The Southern Confederacy
by Eugenia Dunlap Potts
[Read May 11, 1909]

☆ ☆ ☆ ☆

More than a hundred years ago the American States rebelled against the tyranny of England, the mother country, and formed a Confederacy of and among themselves to work together for their own welfare and prosperity. It was granted by their Constitution, and by the States, that each or any individual State had the right under provocation, to withdraw from the pact.

Not quite fifty years ago the Southern States of this Union, having endured provocation after provocation, withdrew from their Northern oppressors, and formed themselves into the Confederacy, whose brief existence ran red with the best blood of her chivalrous land. War was not contemplated. A peaceable separation was desired. A peace conference was held to which representatives of the States were invited. Measure after measure was proposed, so that war might be averted. All were rejected. The recusant States must be whipped back into submission to the autocrats that would direct their affairs. With restricted territory, a minority of population, and home interests directly opposed to those of the over-riding North, what was there to hope for but continuous degradation? Our leaders have been accused of precipitating the war for their own personal ambition. It was another "Aaron Burr conspiracy." Let us hear what they had to say about it.

Jefferson Davis, the fearless soldier and upright citizen – the man who by reason of his supreme fitness was a little later chosen President of the Confederacy, said in his last speech before the United States Senate:

> Secession is to be justified upon the basis that the States are sovereign. When you deny us the right to withdraw from a government which threatens our rights, we but tread in the paths of our fathers when we proclaim our independence. I am sure I but express the feelings of the people whom I represent, toward those whom you represent, when I say I hope, and they hope, for peaceable relations with you, though we must part. This step is taken, not in hostility to others, not to injure any section of the country, not even for our own pecuniary benefit; but from the high and solemn motive of defending and protecting the rights we inherited, and which it is our sacred duty to transmit unshorn to our children.

Alexander Hamilton Stephens, of Georgia, Vice President of the Confederacy, was a Whig, and like others of the leading statesmen, loved the Union. When the North began to control the new territories, and thus denied the South her legitimate share in the Government thereof, Mr. Stephens made a long and powerful argument in the House of Representatives at Washington, some years before the Secession. He said in part:

> If you men of the North, by right of superior numbers, persist in ignoring the claims of the South, sep-

paration must follow; but why not in peace? We say as did the patriarch of old, "Let there be no strife, I pray thee, between me and thee * * * for we be brethren. Is not the whole land before thee? Separate thyself, I pray thee, from me. If thou will take the left hand, then I will go to the right; or if thou depart to the right hand then I will go to the left." In other words if we cannot enjoy this public domain in common, let us divide it. This is a fair proposition. * * * Unless these bitter and sectional feelings of the North be kept out of the National Halls, we must be prepared for the worst. Are your feelings too narrow to make concessions and deal justly by the whole country? Have you formed a fixed determination to carry your measures by numerical strength, and then enforce them by the bayonet? If so the consequences be upon your own head. You may think that the suppression of an outbreak of the Southern States would be a holiday job for a few of your Northern regiments, but you may find to your cost, in the end, that 7,000,000 of people, fighting for their rights, their homes, and their hearthstones, cannot be easily conquered. I submit the matter to your deliberate consideration.

Mr. Stephens, in a speech before the Georgia legislature opposed secession, but said: "Should Georgia determine to go out of the Union, whatever the result may be, I shall bow to the will of my people. Their cause is my cause, and their destiny is my destiny."

These speeches and sentiments do not savor of stirring up strife – of leading the South into rebellion "so that I may be king, and thou my standard bearer." There could be no treason in doing what the Constitution of the United States permitted. And so every speech of farewell made by Southern representatives, was one, first of pleading for redress – then of sincere regret that self-respect and justice forced the rupture. The South never desired war, or bloodshed. The North defied possible war, believing that within a month, at least, any resistance must certainly be conquered. "We can easily whip them back." Well, it was done, but not so easily. Not till years of carnage had wrought their destiny.

John C. Breckinridge, of Kentucky, Vice President of the United States, was termed the arch-traitor of all. His published speeches are in the same spirit of regret, and of affection for the Union. In burning words he showed how the Northern representatives were trampling down the Constitution, and in eloquent remonstrance he pointed the way of escape from threatened disaster. After leaving Congress he entered the Confederate army as Major General, and served as Secretary of War in the cabinet of President Davis.

Robert Toombs, of Georgia, was Secretary of State. In his speech before the U. S. Senate in January, 1861, he reminded his hearers that the Southern States had hundreds of sympathizers among the men of the North, "who respect their oaths, abide by compacts, and love justice."

The brave and patriotic men of the South appealed to the Constitution, they appealed to justice, they appealed to fraternity, until the Constitution, justice, and fraternity were no longer listened to in the legislative halls of their country, and then, sir, they prepared for the arbitrament of the sword. And now you see the glistening bayonet, and you hear the tramp of armed men from your Capitol to the Rio Grand. And all that they have ever demanded is that you abide by the Constitution, as they have done. What is it that we demand? That we may settle in present or acquired territories with our property, including slaves, and that when these territories shall be admitted as States they shall say for themselves whether they wish to have free or slave labor. That is our territorial demand. We have fought for this territory when blood was its price. We have paid for it when gold was its price. New England has contributed very little of blood or money.

The senator goes on to specify what further measures the South demanded, in sharp, incisive terms, but this extract suffices to show that our leaders used every power of tongue and moral suasion to stave off bloodshed.

Houston, Governor of Texas, in a public speech advised constitutional means – anything in reason to prevent war.

Robert E. Lee, the great, the good, was cut to the heart at the impending calamity. One of his friends said: "I have seldom seen a more distressed man." Lee said: "If Virginia stands by the old Union so will I. But if she secedes, then I shall follow my native State with my sword, and, if need be with my life. These are my principles and I must follow them."

Many public men in the North urged peaceable secession, notably, Horace Greeley. Foreign eyes were turned anxiously toward America. The South was sending out millions of pounds of cotton every year, of which the greater part went to England. A London paper of this decade said:

The lives of nearly two million of our country are dependent upon the cotton crops of the States. Should any dire calamity befall the land of cotton, a thousand of our merchant ships would rot idly in dock;

ten thousand mills must stop their busy looms; two thousand mouths would starve for lack of food to feed them.

In 1860, a Southern Senator said in Congress:

There are 5,000,000 of people in Great Britain who live upon cotton. Exhaust the supply one week, and all England is starving. I tell you COTTON IS KING.

But the die was cast. The ordinance of secession of South Carolina unanimously passed December 20, at a quarter past one o'clock. Great crowds were outside the hall of conference awaiting results. The *Charleston Mercury* issued an extra, of which six thousand copies were sold. The chimes of St. Michaels pealed exultant notes; bells of all other churches simultaneously rang. The gun by the post-office christened "Old Secession" belched forth in thundering celebration. Cannons in the citadel echoed the glad tidings; houses and shops emptied their people into the streets; cares of business and family were forgotten; all faces wore smiles – joy prevailed. Old men ran shouting down the streets – friend met friend in hearty hand clasp – the sun shone brilliantly after three days of rain – volunteers donned their uniforms and hastened to their armories. New palmetto flags appeared everywhere. Everyone wore a blue cockade in his hat. Great enthusiasm was shown at the unfurling of a banner on which blocks of stone in an arch typified the fifteen Southern States. These were surmounted by the statue of John C. Calhoun, with the Constitution in his hand, and the figures of Faith and Hope. At the base of the arch were blocks broken in fragments representing the Northern States. A scroll interpreted the allegory to mean a Southern Republic built from the ruins of the other half of the country.

The sentiment of the community was shared by boys firing noisy crackers and Roman candles. The patricians of Charleston drank champagne with their dinners. That night there were grand ceremonies, with military companies, bonfires, and glad demonstrations. The sister States soon caught the infection, and sharing in the hope of independence, they too withdrew from the Union.

On February 4, 1861, delegates from the seceded States – Virginia, Arkansas, Florida, Georgia, North and South Carolina, Mississippi, Texas, Louisiana, Alabama and Tennessee – had met at Montgomery Alabama to organize the Government of the Confederate States. The President and Commander-in-chief, Jefferson Davis, was inaugurated at the State House. Montgomery, February 18, 1861 and again at Richmond, Virginia February 22, 1862.

Inauguration of Jefferson Davis

The Congress of Delegates from the seceding States met at Montgomery, Alabama, on February 4, 1861, and prepared a Provisional Constitution of the new Confederacy. This Constitution was discussed in detail, and was adopted on the 8th. On the next day, February 9, an election was held for the selection of Chief Executive Officers, Jefferson Davis, born in Kentucky, but a resident of Mississippi, being elected President, and Alexander H. Stephens, of Georgia, Vice President. While these important events were transpiring Mr. Davis was at his home, Briarfield, in Mississippi. It was his preference to take active service in the field, but he bowed to the will of his people, and set out for Montgomery to take the oath of office, and assume the tremendous responsibilities to which he had been assigned in the great drama about to be enacted. On his way to Montgomery he passed through Jackson, Grand Junction, Chattanooga, West Point and Opelika. At every principal station along the route he was met by thousands of his enthusiastic fellow-countrymen, clamoring for a speech. During the trip he delivered about twenty-five short speeches, and his reception at Montgomery was an ovation. Eight miles from the capital he was met by a large body of distinguished citizens, and amid the huzzas of thousands and the booming of cannon he entered the city.

From the balcony of the Exchange Hotel he addressed, shortly after his arrival, the immense throng that filled the streets. February 18th had been chosen for the day of the inauguration, and as the time drew near the excitement increased. The ceremony was carried out with all the solemnity and ceremony that could be thrown about it. The military display was a beautiful one, and the martial maneuvers of the troops seemed to portend a victorious issue. A platform was erected in front of the portico of the State House, and standing with uplifted hand on this eminence, while all the approaches were filled with vast crowds of people, Jefferson Davis took the oath of office.

As the hour of noon approached an immense procession was formed, and to the music of fife, drum, and artillery it moved toward the Capitol building. On the platform awaiting the arrival of Mr. Davis were the members of Congress, the President of that body, the Governor of Alabama and Committees, and a number of other distinguished persons. Round after round of cheers greeted Mr. Davis. After being seated on the platform the Rev.

Dr. Manley arose and offered an impressive prayer. President Davis arose and read his inaugural address; then turning, he placed one hand upon the Bible, and with the other uplifted, he listened to the oath. His face was upturned and reverential in expression. At the conclusion of the oath, in solemn, earnest voice, he exclaimed: "So help me God!" He lowered his head in tears, and hundreds wept as they viewed the solemn scene. Thus was officially launched upon a tempestuous sea the Confederate Ship of State.

Order of Procession

Music.

Military Escort of Montgomery Fusileers, Capt. Schenssler; Montgomery Rifles, Capt. Farriss; Eufaula Rifles, Capt. Baker; Columbus (Ga.) Guard, Capt. Sims.

President-Elect, Vice President and Chaplain in an open carriage, drawn by six horses.

Congressional Committee on Ceremonies.

Various Committees.

Commissioners to the Government from States other than the States of the Confederacy.

Ministers of the Gospel, all in carriages.

Citizens in carriages and on foot.

The Department of State, of Justice, the Treasury, War, Navy, Post-office the various military corps, with officers and attaches – all in short, that it takes to form and conduct a government, was ordered from the best picked material. A Constitution was framed like that of the United States, in the main; but the unsatisfactory clauses that had wrought such havoc in the halls of Congress, were changed for the better.

There were in the Confederate service one commander-in-chief, seven generals, nineteen lieutenant-generals, eighty-four major-generals and three hundred and thirteen brigadier-generals. The roster of the Union greatly exceeded these numbers.

When all the departments were organized ready for the administration of the new republic, commissioners were sent to President Lincoln at Washington to negotiate for an equitable transfer of Southern forts, and for terms of an amicable separation. They were refused audience. Every method known to national and international arbitration was attempted without success; so when the strife was precipitated, the South had no resource left but to resist by arms, no matter how overwhelming the odds of the invading section.

On April 12, 1861, General Beauregard, learning that a fleet was forcing its way into Charleston harbor to join Major Anderson at Sumter, opened fire upon the fort. The North charged the war was thus inaugurated by the South. The South believed its action was necessary for self-defence. However that might be, it was the onset of battle – of the greatest Civil War the world has ever known. President Lincoln and President Davis both called for troops. Mass meetings were held in every part of the country North and South. The roll of the drum and the shrill fife of the march were heard in every direction. Muster rolls were drawn up, drills were in progress in hall and on the green. Every youth rushed to take up arms. After the great Confederate victory at Bull Run, some one wrote:

> They have met at last – as storm clouds
> Meet in heaven;
> And the Northmen back and bleeding

Have been driven.
And their thunders have been stilled,
And their leaders, crushed or killed,
And their ranks, with terror thrilled,
Rent and riven.

They had indeed met. And they met and met again. Throughout the length and breadth of the prolific country where cotton was king, the honest achievements of a hundred years were ground into dust by the engines of destruction.

The North came on as invaders; the South stood firm as defenders; and in all the histories of the struggle this fact should be pre-eminent.

Of the hundred battles fought only that of Gettysburg was on Northern soil. The beautiful lands of the garden spot of earth, as I have said, were torn and pillaged and ruined, not alone by the fortunes of civilized warfare, but by the ghastly horrors of cruelty and needless vandalism. It is not the purpose of this paper to fight those battles over. The strife lasted four years. The population of the North was 22,000,000; that of the South 9,000,000, of whom three and one-half millions were slaves. The North was four times as great in numbers as the South.

The North had three times as many armies. The South could not get enough small arms for many months. All foundries for cannon, and all except two powder mills were in the North. The North had food and provisions in abundance. The South planted cotton and tobacco, but could not even in times of peace, raise enough food, but were accustomed to buy from the North and from Europe.

The Union had a treasury and a navy: the Confederacy had neither. The North could renew supplies from abroad. The Southern ports were blockaded and many necessaries of life were shut off. The Confederacy set to work to make arms, ammunitions, blankets, saddles, harness, and other necessities. Bells from churches and halls, dinner bells, plantation and fire bells, along with stray pieces of metal, were melted and cast into cannon. Old nails were saved and blacksmiths made of them clumsy needles, pins and scissors. For coffee was used burnt rye, okra, corn, bran, chickory and sweet potato peelings. For tea, raspberry leaves, corn fodder and sassafras root. There was not enough bacon to be had to keep the soldiers alive. Sorghum was used for sugar.

The women and girls helped in every possible manner. Silk dresses were made into banners, woolen dresses and shawls into soldiers' shirts – carpets into blankets – curtains, sheets, and all linens, were made into lint and bandages for the wounded. Soft white fingers knitted socks, shirts and gloves, to keep the cold from the men in the trenches. Calico was $10 per yard quite early in the strife. Homespun was made upon the old colonial wheels and looms that had been kept as souvenirs and curios. Buttons were obtained from persimmon seeds with holes pierced for eyes. Women plaited their hats from straw or palmetto leaf, and used feathers from barnyard fowls.

One mourning dress would be loaned from house to house as disaster came. Shoes were made of wood, or carriage curtains, buggy tops, saddle tops or any thing like leather. There were thin iron soles like horse shoes. They were patched with bits of old silk dresses. For little children shoes were made from old morocco pocket-books. Flour was $250 per barrel; meal, $50 a bushel; corn, $40 a bushel;

oats, $25; black-eyed peas, $45; brown sugar, $10; coffee, $12; tea, $35 a pound; French merino or mohair sold at $800 to $1,000 a yard; cloth cloak, $1000 and $1500; Balmoral boots, $250 the pair; French gloves, $125 and $150. The stores came to be opened only on occasions.

Salt was the most difficult of all the necessities. The earth from old smoke houses was dug up and boiled for the drippings of ham and bacon – these being crystallized by a primitive process.

Newspapers were printed on coarse half-sheets. Every scrap of blank paper in old note books, letters or waste was utilized. Wall paper and pictures were turned for envelopes. Glue from the peach tree gum served to seal the covers. Poke berries, oak balls, and green persimmons, furnished ink.

The devotion of the people was sublime, always dividing with their neighbors; and the refugees were noted for heroic acts. The negroes were faithful in guarding the families, all of whom were left unprotected, and in working the plantations. Nowhere in the annals of nations has such fidelity been known.

Two negro men belonging to an army officer's widow who lived with her young daughters on an Arkansas plantation, conveyed $50,000 in gold in the cushions of an ambulance to Houston, Texas – a place of safety from marauding troops, who burned the house and cabins, and captured the live stock. The Yankees would not molest escaping negroes. These were faithful to their trust. Similar instances are legion. Leal and true, always and everywhere.

The memory of those hardships cannot die until all the survivors are dead. Fertile fields and pleasant villages were destroyed by great armies. Two billions of dollars in slaves were swept away. Cotton, the chief staple, was burned, or captured. Wealth placed in Confederate bonds, was lost forever. Of the 1,000,000 men in the Southern army, three fourths were killed; 400,000 were crippled; and no estimate was made of the wounded who recovered. The cost of the war was $8,000,000. Men and horses perished of starvation and disease. The Southern Confederacy died, not for lack of the will and of the spirit to fight on – for not even Washington's ragged troops at Valley Forge endured greater sufferings or displayed greater heroism. The Confederacy died of exhaustion.

I have said that the women of the South gave all their energies and ingenuities to the cause. They shared the burdens of conflict. They encouraged and stimulated the men by their sympathy and cheerful fortitude. To their country they gave their dearest and best, and bore up bravely in defeat as well as in victory. With silent courage they faced privation and danger. They nursed the sick and wounded; took charge of farms and plantations. With wonderful resource they supplied the growing deficiencies in domestic affairs. They cared for and directed the thousands of negroes left dependent upon them. They never lost their trust in God, or in the righteousness of their cause though their loved ones languished in prison, or lay dead on the battle field. Their patriotism and womanly fidelity will be held in honor while the world lasts.

And the women refugees from the Border States suffered in addition, the cutting off of news from those they left behind them. Letters went by chance messengers through the lines, or around by Liverpool, England, and finally, by special indulgence, in one-page missives, unsealed, by flag-of-truce, via Newport News and Norfolk, Va.

Sometimes months of silence elapsed. Oftener the

letters were lost. In many cases they straggled in after two, or three years.

Forty-four years have dragged their slow lengths since the last roll-call. We, the survivors and descendants, have buckled on the armor of faithfulness and are honoring the memory of our martyred heroes. We are rearing monuments to perpetuate their deeds of valor. We are cleaning their revered names from aspersion. We are striving to educate the generations to come in the true history of their marvelous struggle for the inalienable rights of every free-born American. How sublime that struggle! How undaunted their attitude! How unsurpassed their fortitude amid the upheaval of their colossal ruin! The conquered banner's tattered folds hang on the wall – her standard-bearer lies in the dust – the sod is green above the heads of her valiant leaders – her rank and file sleep in many an unknown grave. We are in the cooling valleys of peace, where refreshing lies, and above us waves the flag of the old, old Union our people once loved so well. So mote it be. We were loyal to the powers that were; we are loyal to the powers that be. Good citizenship is now, as ever, the watchword of the South. We do not forget our martyrs. Upon our devoted heads rests this sacred duty of consecration. Let us cling together in a cause so noble. Let us merge all thought of self in the glorious work that lies before us.

And what of our beautiful, our historic Southland about which the halo of poesy so lovingly lingers? Nature and man have wrought a mighty restoration. Through the grand old States of Virginia and South Carolina, whose annals contain names which will ever adorn the pages of history, down into the prosperous States of Georgia, Alabama, and Mississippi, through Louisiana, unrivaled in fertility, on to the vast expanse of Texas, whose coming wealth and power may not be measured, there arise prophetic voices from field, forest, mine, and workshop, foretelling the grand stirring into life of extended commerce, enterprise, and capital. Her products have increased and multiplied in kind and in variety, till we hear in the Senate chamber of Congress an eloquent plea for the protection of her interests in the country's political economy. We hear from the lips of the Kentucky Senator a full recognition of our worth, our greatness and alas! the tardy acknowledgment of our *rights*.

These beautiful States are swept by the ocean and mountain winds, and nurtured by the glowing sun and gentle rains. The palmetto and the cypress and the lordly live oak, stand above the glowing orange grove and fragrant magnolia bloom, and the grey moss on the trees, wearing the uniform of the men in grey, wafts a solemn requiem above their narrow beds. The light of prosperity spreads transcendent radiance over the land. The throb of commercial triumph pulsates in the hum of the factory, in the smelting furnace, and ascends in the soft twilight from the rich furrows of her incomparable fields; while the salt sea billows, as they rock her shipping, and dash against pier and wharf, add their exultant voices in prophecy of still greater prosperity.

May advancing wealth rebuild her mansions and fill her coffers, and fittingly crown the efforts of her ambition, and of her genius. May she never lose the aspirations that have made her people through sunshine and storm, a lofty and noble race.

CHAPTER FIVE
Wrongs of History Righted
by Mildred Lewis Rutherford
[delivered Friday, Nov. 13, 1914 at Savannah, Georgia]

☆　☆　☆　☆

My object this evening is not to stress the omissions of history, but rather to urge that some of the wrongs that have already entered history be righted.

We of the South have borne too long and too patiently the many misrepresentations concerning us, and we cannot afford to be patient longer. There is a hope that some of the omissions may enter future history, but what hope can there be of these misrepresentations ever being righted if we neglect to do it now? They have condemned us; they are condemning us; and they will continue to condemn us, if we longer remain indifferent. Let us remember what Dr. Curry said, "If history as now written is accepted it will consign the South to infamy."

When sons and daughters of Veterans write articles for newspapers and magazines, condemning the principles for which their Confederate fathers fought, and even stand for a changed Constitution that will overthrow the very bulwark of the South – State sovereignty – it is full time for the Daughters of the Confederacy and Veterans to become insistent that the truths of history shall be written, and that those truths shall be correctly taught in our schools and colleges.

So long as we send our Southern boys to Harvard to be taught "The Essentials of American History" by Dr. Albert Bushnell Hart, so long may we expect them to question the principles for which their fathers fought. Now understand, I do not object to Dr. Hart, who is a scholar of renown, teaching the Hamiltonian theory of the Constitution to his Northern boys, for that is as they should be taught, but our Southern boys should be sent to Southern universities to be taught the Jeffersonian theory of the Constitution. And so long as we have teachers in our educational institutions who have been taught by Dr. Hart, or by teachers who believe as Dr. Hart teaches, so long may we expect our sons and our daughters to be untrue to the South and the things for which the South stands.

The responsibility is yours, mothers and fathers, to know the training your children are receiving; to know by whom taught, whether true or false to all we hold dear. Only in this way can we stem the tide of falsehoods that have crept in, and are still creeping into the newspapers in our homes, into the books in our libraries, and into the text-books that we are allowing to be used in our schools.

I understand that in one of our leading universities of the South during the past year, two of the professors stated in their classrooms that the South had never produced a great man. Think of it! A section which gave the author of the Bill of Rights, the author of the Declaration of Independence, the author of the United States Constitution, the author of the Monroe Doctrine; a section that gave the commander of the forces of the Revolution, the leaders both on land and on sea of the War of 1812, both leaders of the

War with Mexico, the leaders North and South in the War between the States, and the men most prominent in the Spanish-American War; a section that gave the first President of the United States, indeed gave twelve Presidents to the United States, as well as the President of the Confederate States; a section that gave a Robert E. Lee, and a Stonewall Jackson; a section that gave an Edgar Allan Poe and a Sidney Lanier; a section that gave a Matthew Maury and a Crawford W. Long – yes, a section that gave Woodrow Wilson, the man of the hour and the man of the age, said to have never produced a great man!

Where could these men have been educated but in some anti-South atmosphere! Shall such men as these be allowed to teach the youth of the South true history?

My object to-night is to urge you, Daughters of the Confederacy, to aid in having these wrongs of history righted, and when I urge you to do this, I urge you to do it without bitterness or prejudice or narrowness. As we demand truth and justice, that we must give. Let us be careful to rule out of our Southern textbooks anything that is unjust to the North, and justice compels me to say that wrongs to the North have at times entered into some of our books by Southern writers. Then, too, let us in our search for truth be ever ready to give authority for every statement we make, and require the same of others.

While there are many misrepresentations concerning us in the history which antedates the sixties, yet in my limited time to-night I must confine these misrepresentations to the period which pertains to the War between the States. And, Daughters, I mean the War between the States.

Ours was not a Civil War, so let us correct that wrong first. The United States was a Republic of Sovereign States. We were not a Nation until the surrender left it impossible for a State to secede. A civil war must be in one State between two parties in that State. If we acknowledge that ours was a Civil War, we acknowledge we were a Nation, or one State in 1861 and not a Republic of Sovereign States, and therefore had no right to secede. This is what the North would like us to acknowledge.

It was not a War of Secession as some would have us to call it. The Southern States seceded with no thought of war. They simply wished to have a government where their rights, reserved by the Constitution, should be respected. The war was caused by the North attempting to coerce us back into the Union, contrary to the Constitution, and for no reason save that the States of the South demanded their rights. If we call it a War of Secession we admit the seceding States brought on the war.

It was not a War of Rebellion, for sovereign States cannot rebel, therefore secession was not rebellion. This is acknowledged now by all thinking men.

It was not a War of Sections. The North did not fight the South, for brothers were arrayed against brothers in many cases. There were many men of the South who enlisted on the Union side. There were many men of the North who enlisted on the Southern side. Both North and South were contending for a principle and not because they hated each other.

It was the War between the States, for the non-seceding States made war upon the seceding States to force them back into the Union. Please call it so, and teach it so.

I.
Causes That Led to the War

A wrong to be righted must be the causes that led to the War between the States, for injustice is too often done us by ascribing wrong motives to our secession. These causes far antedate the firing on Fort Sumter, so unfairly said to have begun the war. To really get at the root of the matter, we must go back to that Constitutional Convention in 1787, after the Treaty of Paris had left the Colonies free, sovereign and independent States.

Two political parties were formed at this Convention – the Federalists and Anti-Federalists. The Federalists, standing for a centralized government, were led by Alexander Hamilton, claiming that all States owed allegiance to the Federal Government as the absolute head of the Nation. Now it was perfectly natural for Alexander Hamilton to take this view of the Constitution and think we were a Nation, for he was foreign born – a native of the West Indies. His father and mother before him had served a king, and while he had been sent at an early age to America to be educated, yet this love for and belief in monarchy was an inheritance.

The Anti-Federalists, later called Republicans, but far different from the anti-South party of the same name today, organized in 1854, were led by Thomas Jefferson, standing for local self-government, and the right of any State to withdraw from the Union of States, when a right reserved to it by the Constitution was interfered with. It was perfectly natural for Thomas Jefferson to have this view of the Constitution. The plantation life in the old South made every planter a law to himself, and it was this that has made Southern men ever so tenacious of their State rights. You may say, Thomas Jefferson was in Paris in 1787 and not at that Constitutional Convention. That is true, but he had well instructed Madison, Henry, Randolph and Pinckney concerning the points to be stressed before any new document was signed by Southern States. The Constitution was not fully adopted, you must remember, until after Jefferson's return.

Climate and heredity made the two sections different from the very first – the Northern colonies standing for trade, manufactures, and commerce; the Southern colonies standing for agricultural pursuits and export – but so long as a balance of power was maintained, when voting time came, all went well.

The question of slavery did not enter into the platform of the two parties at all, for all States owned slaves, the right given by the Constitution, and they saw no harm in slavery. It is true the slave trade was a source of deep concern on the part of the majority of the States, and the Southern States seemed really more concerned about this than the Northern. Georgia was the first State to legislate against the slave trade; the Carolinas legislated against it as early as 1760; Virginia, in 1778, and in all "the old Mother State" legislated against it 32 times. Thomas Jefferson's original draft of the Declaration of Independence had a protest against the slave trade, and John Adams of Massachusetts, advised that it be stricken out. Massachusetts was the first State to legislate in favor of the slave trade. New Jersey was the last State to legislate against it, and New York never did legislate against it, so really Massachusetts and New York were carrying on the slave trade in violation of the United States law as late as 1860.

At a glance one may see how unjust have been the accusations concerning the South in regard to the question of slavery. The trouble really between the two political parties was caused by a different interpretation of the Constitution as to what rights were reserved to the States, and whether the Union of States was a Nation or a Republic.

The invention of the cotton gin undoubtedly led to the war. On account of a cold climate, unfavorable to the negro's physical make-up, as well as because manufacturing interests were unsuited to negro labor, the Northern States sold their slaves, in large part to the Southern planters. This gave free labor in the South, and hired labor in the North. Great prosperity came to the South when cotton could be so easily raised and ginned, and there threatened to be an over-balance of voting power by the slave States. Sectional jealousies were engendered and contentions then began.

In 1803 when a Southern President and a slave-holder, Thomas Jefferson, secured the purchase of the Louisiana Territory, that large extent of acres, more than double the area of the other States at that time, Massachusetts was filled with alarm and threatened to secede and form a Northern Confederacy, and Josiah Quincy advised it on sectional grounds. When Jefferson assured them that he was not a President of a section but the President of the whole country, and that he would not violate the Constitution by giving one section an advantage over another, Massachusetts' fears were quieted.

When in 1811 trouble arose about the United States Bank, the legislature of Pennsylvania agitated nullification as justifiable by the Kentucky and Virginia Resolutions. Why later was Calhoun villified for his nullification views? Again, there was trouble in 1812 when the New England States threatened to form a Northern Confederacy if war with England was declared. The South said there would never be freedom from England on sea unless war was declared, and only the great victory at New Orleans prevented the withdrawal of the New England States at that time.

Then in 1820 when Missouri asked to come in as a slave State, and because Missouri was cut out of the Louisiana Territory, Massachusetts feared too much power to slave States and again threatened to withdraw. Thomas, of Illinois, offered a compromise measure to forbid any State above 36° 30" latitude holding slaves. This bill was finally amended to except Missouri. In Northern histories, and Southern histories have followed their lead, it has been over and over again stated, and I have myself often made the same mistake, that Henry Clay was responsible for this amendment. It worried me greatly for it was a direct violation of the U.S. Constitution, and a flagrant interference of States' rights. I hated to think a Southern man was responsible for it. You may imagine my delight when upon reading the *Life of Henry Clay,* I found that he denied having anything to do with it. He was the Speaker of the House at the time and took no part in the debates on the floor. Eminent statesmen of the South felt the injustice of this compromise and did not hesitate to say so. John C. Calhoun never was reconciled to it. But it was finally accepted, just for the sake of peace.

In 1828 and again in 1832 and 1833 Tariff Acts were passed which were unjust to the South and a direct violation of the Constitution, because they favored one section over another. These Acts were such an interference with our States' rights that Calhoun stood for nullifying them – hence he was called "The Nullifier." I have never been able to understand why Calhoun should have been so villified when he proposed a Southern Confederacy at this time and nothing was said when Massachusetts and the New England States proposed a Northern Confederacy.

John C. Calhoun of South Carolina, was one of the real prophets of the age, for everything he warned us against has actually come true, and had we heeded him many valuable lives might have been saved. The "child of secession" was really born in that contest between Robert Y. Hayne of South Carolina and Daniel Webster of Massachusetts, over the Foot Resolutions. The unequal disbursement of the funds in the U.S. Treasury was also felt to be unjust to the South. The South was paying into the treasury two-thirds of all the money there; yet the veterans of the Revolutionary War were paid three times the amount in pensions in the North that they were in the South; the appropriations for roads, harbors, and rivers amounted to five times as much for the North as the South and the money expended for internal improvements ten times as much; twenty-three lighthouses were in the North to ten in the South, and eighteen custom houses in the North to one in the South. The sea coast of the South was 3,000 miles in extent, and that of the North only 900 miles, yet five harbors were in the North to one in the South. Under these circumstances what could the South expect in just legislation?

In 1845 when Texas asked to come into the Union as a slave State, Massachusetts said then she must withdraw, for that would give too much slave territory. When war was declared with Mexico the North had few men comparatively to volunteer and when the cause was won by Southern arms the North, by legislation, tried to manage it so that the South should have no part of the acquired territory as slave territory. In 1847 the Wilmot Proviso was proposed, but fortunately did not become a law, but it showed the tendency of the Northern mind. In 1849 gold was discovered in California and the North wanted it to be a free State. By the Missouri Compromise it should have been half slave territory as half of the State was below the degree of latitude prescribed by the Compromise. Trouble was brewing when "The Peacemaker," Henry Clay, proposed his Omnibus Bill in 1850. This included the "Five Bleeding Wounds," namely:

Let California come in as a free State.

Let Utah and New Mexico come in free or slave as they desire.

Let the slave trade be excluded from the District of Columbia.

Let Texas be paid for the territory claimed by New Mexico.

Let the Fugitive Slave Law be enforced.

Now this virtually repealed the Missouri Compromise, but still it was violating States' rights. However, it was passed in the interest of peace.

While the South knew that some of these measures were unjust, yet to get back her slaves, for at this time 30,000 had been hidden from their owners, she was willing to adopt the compromise measures that grew out of this bill. Many Southern statesmen protested against it, and it only postponed the war ten years.

In 1852 *Uncle Tom's Cabin* appeared. This was such a misrepresentation of the institution of slavery in the South that it brought just indignation to Southern people. It was so subtly written that it made the abolition sentiment stronger at the North, and really had much to do in bringing on the war and much to do in keeping England, France and other European countries from recognizing the Southern Confederacy. The South felt this injustice keenly.

Then in 1854 the Kansas-Nebraska Bill proposed

by Stephen Douglas passed. This led to Squatter Sovereignty, another violation of the Constitution and an interference with our States' rights. There is no doubt that John Brown's Raid grew out of this bill. The first gun fired in this raid may be said to have been the first gun of the War between the States.

John Brown was "an insurrectionist, an invader of States, an encourager of arson, and a murderer" – and this is quoting entirely from Northern authority. I could never understand how God-fearing men from the pulpits in the North have said that next to the Son of God, John Brown was the greatest of martyrs. It has taken all the grace of Christianity for the South to forgive and forget this. However, the Federal Government quickly punished this offender, and also decided in favor of the South when the Dred Scott case came to trial. So we began to take hope that at last the South could fall back upon her reserved rights and be protected.

Another offense then came. The slave trade was being openly violated and no action was taken by the Federal Government to prevent it. It had been decided by law that the slave trade should cease in 1808, and yet as late as 1857 it was known that 75 slave ships had sailed from Massachusetts ports, and between 1859 and '60, it was known that 85 slave ships left New York, sent out by merchants carrying 60,000 slaves to Brazil. As late as 1857 the *Chlotilde* was sent to Mobile, Ala., with 175 slaves, and the following year the New York Yacht Club sent the *Wanderer* to Brunswick, Ga., with 750 slaves, and the next year it returned with 600 slaves and sailed up the Satilla and Savannah rivers and sold this cargo in violation of the law. An attempt was made by Georgia to prosecute two Georgians who were accused of encouraging the transaction, but they could not be convicted for complicity in the scheme. If the Federal Government ever punished Massachusetts and New York for violating the law it is not so recorded.

But the act which brought things to a crisis was the election of Abraham Lincoln as President of the United States, without even a popular vote of the North, but by the vote of the fifteen States which had stood for these repeated violations of the Constitution and continued interferences with States' rights, and the States which took out the "Personal Liberty Bills," advocating a law higher than the Constitution so that they might still hide our slaves. By this time (1860), 50,000 slaves had been hidden from us. Unfortunately the Democratic party split, having three candidates in the field – a warning that we must hereafter heed – and allowed Lincoln to be elected on the small vote of 1,831,000, There was nothing for the South to do but to secede. She saw nothing but continued violation of the Constitution by the North dominated by the policy of these fifteen States and their candidate. How could she be blamed for seceding?

Did the Southern States secede with any thought of war? No, they simply wished to peacefully withdraw and form a government which would respect their rights as reserved by the Constitution. It would have been a stupid thing for seven States to think of fighting all of the other States in the Union. The North had the army; the North had the navy; the North had all of the arms. The South had no arms except the small number of guns that Secretary Floyd had asked for, fearing another John Brown might arise, and those Jefferson Davis, when Secretary of War, had asked for to quell the Indian uprisings. Even then the full quota of arms which rightly be-

longed to the South had never been asked for.
Does it not seem in reason, if the South had had
a thought of war at this time she would have demanded
her full share of arms and ships? The South had no materials
to manufacture munitions of war. That is, she did not know
that she had sulphur, salt pretre, nitre and other needful
things lying undiscovered beneath her soil, but she knows
it now; she then had few manufactories; she only had one
Powder Mill, that at Augusta, Ga.; she did not own a ship,
yet her Southern men in command of ships, (there were
43 captains and 62 commanders in all from the South,) when
the States seceded, surrendered their commissions to the
U.S. Government and came home to cast their lot with their
States. Had they dreamed of war, they could have brought
their ships South as they had a right to do. She did not have
a ship-yard where a ship could even be repaired. She had
only 9,000,000 people from which to draw an army, and
4,000,000 of these were her slaves, while the North had
over 31,000,000 and the whole world from which to draw
recruits. Think of war? No, she never dreamed of it. Some
few of her statesmen feared it, but when suggested, Robert
Toombs of Georgia, said he would willingly drink every
drop of blood which would be shed by war.

The South only desired to take possession of the
things which were rightfully hers. Texas demanded her
forts and arsenal so did Louisiana her custom house and
fort; Mississippi, Alabama, Florida and Georgia their forts
and arsenals; but when South Carolina demanded Fort
Sumter, to the surprise of South Carolina, it was refused.
Governor Pickens at once sent a request to President Buchanan to allow the fort to be surrendered peaceably.
Assurances were given that this would be, and yet the
Star of the West was sent with 200 men and arms to hold

the fort. The first thing that the Confederate Government did was to send a committee of three to Washington to ask the peaceable surrender of Fort Sumter. They waited there three months until President Lincoln had been inaugurated and then made the request. He refused to see the committee, but through Seward, and Seward through Judge Campbell, sent to them assurances that "faith with Fort Sumter would be kept." Now Lincoln and Seward both knew that when this message was sent, seven vessels filled with armed men had already sailed to garrison the fort. When time sufficient had elapsed for the vessels to land, then Lincoln wired Gov. Pickens that he had sent these men to Sumter peacefully if allowed to land, otherwise resistance would be made. Fortunately a storm prevented the vessels reaching the fort as soon as had been expected, so Gen. Beauregard telegraphed for permission to demand the surrender of the fort. This permission was granted by the Confederate Government. Anderson said he must wait for orders from headquarters. Beauregard answered that if the fort was not surrendered by a certain time it would be fired upon. It was not surrendered, so was fired upon. The firing of the first shot at Fort Sumter did not bring on the war, but the act which made the firing necessary declared war. The call of President Lincoln for 75,000 troops to coerce the South, without Congress' consent, was a violation of the Constitution. Virginia, North Carolina, Tennessee and Arkansas resented this and quickly seceded. Missouri, Kentucky and Maryland wished to secede but were not allowed to vote on secession. This act of Lincoln calling for troops was in itself a declaration of war.

Was secession rebellion? The very fact that President Davis and the leaders of the South could not be brought to trial disproves this. Chief Justice Chase said, "If you bring these leaders to trial it will condemn the North, for by the Constitution secession is not rebellion." Wendell Phillips said, and he was no friend of the South, "Looking back upon the principles of '76 the South had a perfect right to secede." Horace Greely said so, Lincoln himself said so, and Daniel Webster had said so.

I wonder how many here present realize that there have been eight distinct secessions in the United States and very many threatened ones.

1. The 13 colonies seceded from England and formed a Perpetual Union under the Articles of Confederation in 1776.

2. The 13 States seceded from the Perpetual Union and formed a Republic of Sovereign States in 1787.

3. Texas seceded from Mexico and became a Republic in 1836.

4. The Abolitionists, led by William Lloyd Garrison, seceded from the Constitution at Framingham, Mass., and publicly burned it, calling it a "league with hell and covenant with death," the assembled multitude loudly applauding.

5. Eleven States seceded from the Union in 1861 and formed a Southern Confederacy.

6. The North seceded from the Constitution in 1861 when she attempted to coerce the eleven States back into the Union.

7. Under President McKinley in 1889 the United States forced Cuba to secede from Spain.

8. Under Roosevelt in 1905 the United States forced Panama to secede from Colombia.

Why should all of these secessions be justifiable save the one by the South in 1861?

Was the war fought to hold our slaves? Ah! how often have we of the South had this cast into our teeth and often by some of our own Southern people. Yes, it is full time this wrong should be righted.

Had the vote been taken in 1860 there would have been more votes against the abolition of slavery in the North than in the South. There were 318,000 slaveholders or sons of slaveholders in the Northern army, men who enlisted from the Border States, Missouri, Kentucky, Tennessee, Maryland, besides those from Illinois, Pennsylvania, New Jersey and Delaware. There were only 200,000 slaveholders in the Southern army. Only five men out of every one hundred owned slaves in the South.

There were many men among the leaders of the Northern army who owned slaves themselves or were sons of slaveholders or had married women who owned slaves. Among these may be mentioned Gen. Winfield Scott, Commodore Farragut, Gen. George H. Thomas, Gen. Grant; Pres. Lincoln's wife came from a slaveholding family, and Stephen Douglas's wife was a very large slaveholder, while many of the leaders on the Southern side did not own slaves. Gen. Lee had freed his. Gen. Stonewall Jackson never had owned one until husband and wife begged him to buy them to prevent separation. Gen. Albert Sidney Johnston never owned a slave, and Gen. William M. Browne, a member of Pres. Davis's staff, never owned a slave. No, the war was not fought to hold slaves, but a few selfish Southern people may have thought so.

Gen. Grant said, "If I thought this war was to abolish slavery, I would resign my commission and offer my sword to the other side." The North had no thought of fighting to abolish slaves, then why should the South be troubled on that score? Pres. Lincoln sent word to Gen.

Butler that the war was not to be fought with any idea of freeing the slaves. Pres. Lincoln was only concerned about the extension of slavery in the new territory, and frankly confessed to Horace Greeley that if the Union could be preserved with slavery he would not interfere with it. It was the preservation of the Union he so ardently desired. He had no love for the negro in his heart. Donn Piatt who stumped the State of Illinois for him in his presidential campaign in 1860, said in one of his speeches that Lincoln had no love for the negro: "Descended from the poor whites of the South he hated the negro and the negro hated him, and he was no more concerned for that wretched race than he was concerned for the horse he worked or the hog he killed."

II.
Slavery

Was slavery a crime and was the slaveholder a criminal? How little the people living today know of the institution of slavery as it existed in the South before the war. I long for the eloquence of our silver-tongued orator, Benjamin H. Hill, that I might paint the picture as I remember it.

If the roll call were taken of the children in the South today they would in large numbers be found to be abolitionists, intense and fanatical, and in full sympathy with the Northern side. Why? Because from childhood they have been taught by teachers who believe this, and have been fed on such children's books as "The Elsie Books," Louisa Alcott's stories, and kindred ones, besides being allowed to see moving picture shows of *Uncle Tom's Cabin, Sheridan's Ride, Contest Between*

Merrimac and Monitor, and the like. Whom can you blame for this, parents, but yourselves?

Slavery was no disgrace to the owner or the owned. From time immemorial all civilized nations had been slaveholders. White, brown and black have been slaves.

Who was responsible for slavery in the United States? Spain and England.

What colony first owned slaves? The Jamestown colony.

Was there any colony or State of all the thirteen which did not own slaves? Not one. In 1776 there were 500,000 slaves in America and 300,000 were in the Northern colonies.

What was the condition of the Africans when brought to this country? Savage to the last degree, climbing cocoanut trees to get food, without thought of clothes to cover their bodies, and sometimes cannibals, and all bowing down to fetishes – sticks and stones – as acts of worship.

What laws became necessary when they reached this country? Very rigid and, in the light of present day civilization, excessively cruel. A strong argument for the civilizing power of slavery would be to compare these colonial laws with the laws of 1860.

How did the Cavaliers regard slavery? They were very thankful to have a part in such a wonderful missionary and educational enterprise.

How did the Puritans regard slavery? They thanked God for the opportunity of bringing these benighted souls to a knowledge of Jesus Christ.

How did the Quakers regard the institution of slavery? They were always opposed to the holding of any human being as property, although it is stated that William

Penn did once own slaves.

Does the Bible condemn slavery?

It certainly does not. God gave to Abraham the most explicit directions what he should do with his slaves bought with his own money, and what he should do with the ones he owned by right of capture. (Gen. 17). Then our Lord healed the centurion's servant and said not a word about it being a sin to hold him in bondage. (Matt. 8). And Paul sent Onesimus, the runaway slave, back to his master with apologies, but said nothing to Philemon about freeing him, but rather offered himself to pay his master for the time Onesimus had stolen from him. (Phil. 1, 18). And Titus was the pastor of a slave church. Paul wrote to him to exhort those slaves to be obedient to their masters, not to answer back again, and not to steal, but to adorn the doctrine of God their Savior in all things. (Titus 2 :9, 10). See also Eph. 6:5, 6, 7, 8.

Did the slaveholder in the South take an interest in the religious condition of the negro?

He certainly did. More negroes were brought to a knowledge of God and their Savior under this institution of slavery in the South than under any other missionary enterprise in the same length of time. Really more were Christianized in the 246 years of slavery than in the more than thousand years before.

In 1861 there were, by actual statistics, in the seceding States 220,000 negro Baptists, 200,000 Methodists, 31,000 Presbyterians, 7,000 Episcopalians, and 30,000 belonging to unclassified Christian churches.

The negro race should give thanks daily that they and their children are not today where their ancestors were before they came into bondage.

Was the negro happy under the institution of slavery?

They were the happiest set of people on the face of the globe, – free from care or thought of food, clothes, home, or religious privileges.

The slaveholder felt a personal responsibility in caring for his slaves physically, mentally, morally, and spiritually. By the way, we never called them slaves; they were our people, our negroes, part of our very homes. I do not remember a case of consumption, or I should say now tuberculosis, among the negroes in the South. I do not recall but one crazy negro in those days. Hospitals and asylums cannot now be built fast enough to accommodate them.

I am not here to defend slavery. I would not have it back, if I could, but I do say I rejoice that my father was a slave-holder, and my grandfathers and great-grand-fathers were slave-holders, and had a part in the greatest missionary and educational endeavors that the world has ever known. There never have been such cooks, such nurses or mammies, such house-maids, such seamstresses, such spinners, such weavers, such washer women. There never have been such carpenters, blacksmiths, butlers, drivers, field hands, such men of all work as could be found on the old plantations. Aunt Nanny's cabin was a veritable kindergarten where the young negroes were trained to sew, to spin, to card, to weave, to wash and iron, and to nurse; where the boys were taught to shell peas, to shuck corn, to churn, to chop wood, to pick up chips, to feed pigs, to feed chickens, to hunt turkey, duck, guinea, goose and hen eggs and to make fires, and to sweep the yards.

Did the negroes hate their owners, and resent bondage? I need only to call to mind what happened when John Brown tried to make them rise and murder their masters and their masters' children. I need only call to mind what happened when their, masters went to battle, leaving in absolute trust "ole Mis" and the children to their protection. I need only call to mind what happened after they were free that made Thad Stevens' Exodus Order necessary in order to tear them from their old owners. I need only call to mind the many mammies who stayed to nurse "Ole Marster's" children to the third and fourth generation.

Compare the race morally to what it was then. "Ole Marster" never allowed his negroes to have liquor unless he gave it to them. Crimes now so common were never known then. While the negro under the present system of education may know more Latin and Greek, it does not better fit him for his life work. It is true the negro did not go to school under slavery, but he was allowed to be taught, if he so desired. I have in mind a young aunt who taught three negro women every night because they wanted to read their Bibles. I have in mind my mother on the plantation surrounded every Sunday afternoon teaching to the negro children the same verses of Scripture, the same Sunday School lesson, the same hymns that she taught her own children.

As in family life a child must be punished if disobedient, so in plantation life a negro had to be punished if disobedient. Even admitting that some overseers were cruel, will the most exaggerated cases of cruelty compare with the burning of the witches at Salem or the awful conditions of the captured Africans on the slave ships, or the fearful conditions in the sweatshops of Chicago and New York today? The slave was the property of the slaveholder and a selfish reason would have protected him if there had been no higher motive.

No, the slaveholder was no criminal and slavery

under the old regime was no crime. In all the history of the world no peasantry was ever better cared for, more contented or happier.

These wrongs must be righted and the Southern slaveholder defended as soon as possible.

III.
Jefferson Davis vs. Abraham Lincoln.

Another wrong that must be righted is this glorification of Abraham Lincoln which redounds to the villification of Jefferson Davis. Our children are having too much of it in their text-books, too much of it in the newspapers, too much of it from the pulpits.

Had President Davis died in that cold, damp cell with manacles upon him, and had President Lincoln lived, Davis would have been the saint and Lincoln, the sinner. It is not fair or just because Lincoln was the martyr that attributes which he did not possess should be given to him and handed down as truthful history.

I am perfectly willing to have President Lincoln receive the praise he justly deserves, for he was a remarkable man, and I would not detract one iota from what is his due. At the same time I am not willing to ascribe attributes to President Davis which he did not possess, for he was remarkable enough without them. Both men had their weaknesses and neither should be canonized.

Lest I should be accused of partiality when their lives are placed in parallel lines, I shall only quote from the friends of each. Both had enemies, vindictive and prejudiced; both had friends, loyal and true. This contrast truthfully and faithfully drawn will throw much light upon unwritten history. If injustice to either has been done, it

has not come from any desire or intention on the part of the historian, for it is truth only that is sought.
Jefferson Davis was born in Christian Co., Kentucky, June 3rd, 1808.
Abraham Lincoln was born in Hardin Co., Ky., Feb. 12, 1809.
There was a difference of eight months in their ages; they were born about 100 miles apart in the same State – both men Kentuckians of Southern birth.
Jefferson Davis came from a home of culture, refinement, luxury, and religious influence.
Abraham Lincoln came from a home of poverty, no refinement, no culture and little religious influence.
Jefferson Davis had every educational advantage in youth. His first teacher was a loving, devoted Christian mother. He was then sent to an academy, then to college, then to West Point. His ambition was to become a great military leader.
Abraham Lincoln lost his mother when quite young. He attended school for a very short time. Thomas Lincoln's second wife was a very good woman and treated the lad kindly. He was sent from home at the age of nine, and then began the struggle for life. He did all kinds of hard work; he split rails, he worked on a ferry, he clerked in a store, and had no time for study except at night after a hard day's work. Often no light by which to study save the light from the fire. His ambition made him struggle on to acquire an education under the most adverse circumstances. His desire was to become a great political leader, and if possible the President of the United States.
Jefferson Davis in personal appearance was tall, erect, lean, with features very pronounced, and determi-

nation stamped on every lineament. He was always well groomed, perfectly a tease in his manners whether in the cabin of the lowly, the home of the wealthy, or the White House of the Confederacy. He always enjoyed social life.

Abraham Lincoln was tall, with stooping shoulders, thin and bony, with prominent features but with determination written upon every lineament. He was never well dressed, his clothes having the appearance of being thrown at him. He was always ill at ease, whether in the cabin of the lowly, the home of the wealthy, or the White House of the United States. He hated social life, if possible, avoided it.

Jefferson Davis had little humor in his nature and resented a practical joke. Life was always very serious to him. He was dignity personified, and his soldierly bearing forbade even his most intimate friends getting very close to him.

Abraham Lincoln loved jokes, indulged in them very frequently and often his jokes were none too refined. His friends felt very near to him and enjoyed thoroughly his humor.

Jefferson Davis was very happy in his married life. His first wife was the daughter of Pres. Zachary Taylor, his second wife was Miss Varina Howell, the daughter of a United States officer. His home was in Mississippi on a large plantation, surrounded by every comfort to make his life a joy. Children came into the home-nest and his children were obedient, talented and loving. Sorrow later came from the loss of two of his boys, but he knew the source of comfort and did not rebel.

Abraham Lincoln's married life was not happy. He had three romances connected with his early days. One, Amy Rutledge, belonged to his own social circle. Had he married her possibly his whole life would have been changed, but unfortunately she died while attending school. His other loves were Mary Owens and Mary Todd. He really loved neither, but in turn addressed each, became engaged to both, but advised both not to marry him, as he did not belong to their social set. It is said that Mary Owens jilted him, which greatly mortified him, but Mary Todd agreed to marry him. The day, January 1, 1842, was appointed, the bride and attendants were waiting at the church, but no bridegroom appeared. It is said that his most intimate friends were never able to account for Lincoln's behavior upon this occasion. Mary Todd forgave him, however, and married him one year later. It was a most unfortunate marriage for she was not suited to make him happy, and while children came into the home there was no real joy, for that can only come from a perfectly congenial atmosphere. He, too, lost one of his sons while living at Springfield, Ill., and he became very morose and melancholy, for Herndon and Lamon both said Lincoln had no Christian faith to sustain him.

Jefferson Davis was a slaveholder, and his father before him owned slaves. He was a kind master and his negroes were devoted to him. Even after they were free, when their former master returned home from two years' confinement in prison, they climbed about his carriage, calling to him affectionately, "Howdy, Mars Jeff, howdy. We sho is glad to see you." Then falling back and wiping the tears from their eyes they were heard to say, "Lord, don't he look bad."

The testimony of his body servant who was with him when captured, if we did not have that of Judge Reagan and other of the cabinet members, would be sufficient to refute the awful falsehood of Gen. Wilson's telegram, that he was disguised in a woman's dress when arrested. This faithful servant said, "When we heard the Yankees coming we was skeered to death, but old Boss he walked just as straight as if he was walking the streets of Richmond with Lee and Jackson. He was the bravest man I ever saw. I was sho the Yankees was going to hang him, but if he ever flinched nobody ever saw him. Folks may say what they please, but Mars Jeff sho was brave."

Abraham Lincoln belonged to the poor white class in the South, who hated the negroes and they hated them. He was no abolitionist, and this is from his own testimony. His wife came from a slave holding family but probably owned no slaves at the time of her marriage.

Both men served in the Black Hawk War. Lieut. Davis mustered into service Capt. Abraham Lincoln of the militia. Neither distinguished himself in any way during this war.

Davis later entered the Mexican War and won great renown. At Monterey he was wounded, at Buena Vista he was a hero, and later led the troops into Mexico City with great bravery. In his military life he was known as a fine disciplinarian, and while his soldiers feared him and dared not disobey him, they thoroughly respected him.

Jefferson Davis ran for the legislature and was defeated, afterwards was elected, became U. S. senator, then a member of Pres. Pierce's Cabinet, as Secretary of War. He successfully reorganized the army, and was the first to suggest the trans-continental railway. He then became U. S. Senator under Pres. Buchanan, and made a very strong speech on State Sovereignty. When he heard his State, Mississippi, had seceded he returned to cast in his lot with her. He was made Major General of the army, just what he most desired. When the Provisional Congress

of the Confederate States met at Montgomery, Ala., he
was chosen President without opposition. He did not seek
or desire this honor, but ever went where duty called him.
Abraham Lincoln also ran for the legislature and
was defeated, but afterwards elected. He became a member of Congress in 1846. Then in 1860 was a candidate
for U.S. President on the Republican ticket upon an anti-
South platform, and was elected.

President Davis served one year as President of
the Confederacy, was reelected for the second term of six
years and did the best he could combating overwhelming
odds. When Gen. Lee surrendered, he was rapidly making
his way to join the last division of the army under Kirby
Smith in Texas, when he was captured at Irwinton, Ga.,
and taken prisoner to Fortress Monroe to await trial. A
reward of $100,000 was offered for his capture. He was
put in chains and treated with great indignities. Is it to be
wondered at that he fell to the floor when the blacksmith
who came in to rivet the chains? He remained in prison
two years. The United States authorities did not heed the
requests from Judge Reagan of Texas, and Gen. Howell
Cobb of Georgia, for an immediate trial, which they knew
would exonerate him, or greater leniency in the treatment
of him. When it was discovered that a trial would condemn the North, by a statement from Chief Justice Chase
to this effect, he was released from prison under bond,
and Horace Greeley said, "I will give his bond that the
North may seem to be magnanimous." He returned to his
home at Beauvoir, Miss., a gift from a devoted friend and
admirer Mrs. Sarah Dorsey. There he lived until his death
which occurred in New Orleans in 1889. He was buried
in New Orleans, and his body later removed to Richmond, Va.

As Bishop Gailor said:

> For twenty years he bore the obloquy of treason at the hands of those who were afraid to try him in a court of justice. For twenty years he was disfranchised and denied the rights of citizenship. Yet he never sued for pardon, nor ever asked a favor. Lonely and crushed, with a heart broken, his life was desolated in its prime. But through it all God gave him the courage of the finest manhood, and the purest purpose, and he died, as he lived, a Christian, praying for the welfare and happiness of his people. Truly he was a man without a country, yet he had a country in the hearts of his loyal Southern people – and in that country he ruled an unconquered king.

The soldiers who had not agreed with him in many things during the war realized later what he had borne for the South, and turned to him then in loving affection. At Macon, the last reunion that he was able to attend, some of the soldiers thrust into his hands an old tattered and torn battle flag. Taking it in both hands he buried his face in its folds. Strong men sank to the ground and leaned on each other's shoulders weeping like children. They felt then, as they feel now, that while the cause was not lost, the principles for which they con-tended being admitted constitutional by all right thinking men the world over, the life of their chief had been sacrificed for it, and their hearts were breaking.

Abraham Lincoln was afraid to go to Washington, so said his friend Lamon, so intense was the feeling against him; this feeling he feared more from his enemies at the North than at the South. Lamon, as a detective, accompanied the President who insisted upon going in disguise. His friends felt this was a cowardly thing to do and reproached him for it. He served four years and was reelected over McClellan for another term, then he was foully assassinated by John Wilkes Booth. His body was carried to Springfield, Ill. President Davis's first exclamation upon hearing the news was, "This is the worst blow that could have befallen the South."

IV.
Political Differences.

There was a very striking likeness in many ways between these two men which has led some to falsely suggest some degree of kinship between them.

Both believed in the constitutional rights of the States.

Both believed in the right to hold slaves by the Constitution.

Both were opposed to social and political equality for the negro.

Both believed it would be disastrous to free negroes among their former masters.

Both believed only in educating the negro along industrial lines.

Both believed in the preservation of the Union, if possible.

Lincoln believed and urged the colonization of the negro; Davis believed in the gradual emancipation of the negro. He thought the South was the logical home of the black man, and that the Southern people better understood him and were most ready to make excuses for his short comings. He believed that in the South the negro could always find sympathy, protection, religious instruction, work and a home.

It has always seemed to me that when birthdays are being celebrated in the South, the negroes had far better celebrate Davis's birthday than Lincoln's. He was their truest friend. Besides, it was Henderson's 13th Amendment after Lincoln's death that freed them. Lincoln's Emancipation Proclamation did not free all the negroes and was only made to punish the seceding States. The negroes have been kept in such ignorance along these lines, and their false worship of Lincoln is pathetic.

Did Pres. Davis have any trouble with his Cabinet? He certainly did. Alexander Stephens, his Vice-President, frequently disagreed with him. Some of his cabinet resigned. Some accused him of being imperious and partial. George Vest said, "Had Davis's Cabinet stood by him notwithstanding they did not agree with him, the Confederacy would not have failed." Some of Pres. Davis's generals felt that he favored pointedly West Point men over others better fitted to command.

Did Lincoln have trouble with his Cabinet? He certainly did, Ben Wade and Henry W. Davis issued a manifesto against him. Sumner, Wade, Davis, and Chase were his "malicious foes." Lincoln was forced to appoint Chase to the office of Chief Justice in order to remove him from the cabinet, for he was said to be "the irritating fiy in the Lincoln ointment." Stanton called Lincoln "a coward and a fool." Seward said he had "a cunning that amounted to genius." Richard Dana said, "The lack of respect for the President by his Cabinet cannot be concealed." He was called "the baboon at the other end of the avenue," and "the idiot of the White House." Had not Grant succeeded in gaining a victory at Vicksburg, a movement to appoint a dictator in Lincoln's place would have gone into effect. His Cabinet had lost confidence in his policy.

Was Davis honest and true to his convictions? If by honesty is meant taking graft or accepting bribes, he certainly could never have been accused of either. If by honesty is meant true to any principle which he knew to be right, whether it was expedient or not, he most undoubtedly was honest, and true to his convictions.

Was Abraham Lincoln honest and true to his convictions? If by being honest you mean taking graft and accepting bribes, he certainly was honest, and won the title of "Honest Abe." But if by being honest is meant true to the things he believed, then Lincoln was not.

He wrote Alexander Stephens before he was inaugurated that the slaves would be as safe under his administration as they were under that of George Washington. Did he change his mind when expedient? He told a friend in Kentucky that if he would vote for him every fugitive slave should be returned. Was it expedient to return any? At Peoria, Ill., in 1854 he said, "I acknowledge the constitutional rights of the States – not grudgingly, but fairly and fully, and I will give them any legislation for reclaiming their fugitive slaves." Did he? He said the slaveholder had a legal and a moral right to his slaves. Was he honest when he violated the Constitution by freeing some of them?

He believed at one time it would not be constitutional to coerce the States, and then later he believed it would. A friend asked why he changed his mind. He replied, "If I allow the South to secede whence will come my revenue?"

In 1848 and in 1860 Lincoln said the Southern States had a right to secede; in 1861 he said they would be traitors and rebels if they did secede.

No, Lincoln's convictions of right or wrong changed whenever expedient.

Did President Davis ever violate the Constitution? If he did his worst enemies have never been able to discover it. Secession was not a violation of the U.S. Constitution. When a President of the United States offered to give him the highest office in militia military service, an honor he most desired, he refused because he said that was a gift from the State, not the Government.

Did Lincoln ever violate the Constitution? Sumner said when Lincoln reinforced Fort Sumter, and called for 75,000 men without the consent of Congress, it was the greatest breach ever made in the Constitution and would hereafter give any President the liberty to declare war whenever he wished without the consent of Congress. In his inaugural address, Lincoln said he had no intention to interfere with the slaves, for the South had a legal right by the Constitution to hold them. Why then did he issue his Emancipation Proclamation to free the South's slaves? Did he not violate the Constitution when he sanctioned the formation of West Virginia, a new State taken from Virginia, without Virginia's consent? Did he not violate the Constitution when he suspended the writ of *habeas corpus*, May 10, 1861 in the Merriman case? Yes, Lincoln violated the Constitution whenever he desired.

Was Jefferson Davis humane? He certainly was. When the soldiers were returning victorious from the first Battle of Manassas, and President Davis went out to meet them, he said that he commended their humane treatment of those 10,000 prisoners of war as much as he commended their valor, great as it was. When he was urged to retaliate for alleged cruelties to our prisoners at the North, his reply was, "The inhumanity of the enemy to our prisoners can be no justification for a disregard by us of the rules of civilized war and Christianity." The *Richmond Examiner* said that this humane policy of the President would be the ruin of the Confederacy. His heart went out in agony over the suffering of the Andersonville prisoners, and his inability to help them because of the refusal to exchange prisoners, and to send medicines.

Was Abraham Lincoln humane? When Alexander Stephens, a personal friend, went on to Washington to plead for a renewal of the cartel to exchange prisoners, owing to a congested condition at Andersonville beyond the power of the Confederate Government to relieve, he put this request on the score of humanity and friendship, not as a political measure; the request was refused. When President Davis, Col. Ould and Gen. Howell Cobb pleaded for an exchange of prisoners at Andersonville on the plea of mercy, as the stockade was overcrowded and the water conditions bad, was the request granted? When six of the prisoners were paroled in order to go to Washington to plead for exchange, was their request even given a fair hearing? When Col. Ould begged that medicines which had been made contraband of war should be sent to their own surgeons to use only for their own men, was not that request denied? When Col. Ould asked that a vessel be sent to take the sick and wounded home, because of the lack of room, lack of cooking vessels to prepare the food and lack of medicines to give proper attention, it was refused, unless 1500 men were sent to them. Word was returned that the vessel would be filled with well men to complete that number, and although this answer went in August it was December before the vessel was sent, and that after many, many had died. When Gen. Cobb sent the prisoners to Florida, the Federal officers refused to receive them, but they were left there anyway. Was Sheridan's treatment of the women and children in the Valley of the Shenandoah, or Sherman's treatment of them in Atlanta, or in his March through Georgia, or at the burning of Columbia, or Butler's treatment of the women in New Orleans humane? Yet Lincoln as Commander-in-Chief of the army allowed it and never once reproved it. No, Lincoln was not humane. Nevertheless this quality has been given to him in full measure since his martyrdom.

Did Lincoln intend to free the slaves when war was declared? Certainly he did not. In his speech at Peoria, Ill., he said:

Free them and keep them here as underlings? That would not better their condition.

Free them and make them socially and politically our equals? My own feelings will not admit this, and I know the mass of whites North and South will not agree to this. We cannot make them our equals.

Free them and send them to Liberia would be my first impulse, but I know if they were landed there today they would perish in ten days.

If all earthly power were given to me I do not know what to do with slavery as it exists in the South today.

A system of gradual emancipation seems best, and we must not too quickly judge our brethren of the South for a seeming tardiness in this matter.

Does this seem that he had the Emancipation Proclamation or anything like it in his mind at that time? Was Lincoln magnanimous? Yes, Lincoln was magnanimous, for there is no doubt that Grant's magnanimity to Lee was Lincoln's thought, not Grant's. One who was present when

Grant went to consult Lincoln about this testifies to this fact.

Was Lincoln highly extolled by his friends Herndon and Lamon before his martyrdom? No, they saw many faults in their friend Lincoln which were quickly expunged from later editions of their books. The first copies of these books were rapidly destroyed. Rare copies of them are, however, still to be found.

What were Lincoln's views about colonization? From the time of his election as President he was striving to find some means of colonizing the negroes. An experiment had been made of sending them to Liberia, but it was a failure, and he wished to try another colony, hoping that would be successful. He sent one colony to Cow Island under Koch as overseer, but he proved very cruel to the negroes and they begged to return. He then asked for an appropriation of money from Congress to purchase land in Central America, but Central America refused to sell and said, "Do not send the negroes here." The North said, "Do not send the negroes here," It was then agreed that a Black Territory should be set apart for the segregation of the negroes in Texas, Mississippi and South Carolina – but Lincoln was unhappy, and in despair he asked Ben Butler's advice, saying, "If we turn 200,000 armed negroes in the South among their former owners from whom we have taken their arms, it will inevitably lead to a race war. It cannot be done. The negroes must be gotten rid of." Ben Butler said, "Why not send them to Panama to dig the canal?" Lincoln was delighted at the suggestion, and asked Butler to consult Seward at once. Only a few days later John Wilkes Booth assassinated Lincoln and one of his conspirators wounded Seward. What would have been the result had Lincoln lived cannot be estimated. The poor negroes would possibly have been sent to that place of yellow fever and malarial dangers to perish from the face of the earth, for we had no Gorgas of Alabama to study our sanitary laws for them at that time.

By the way, another wrong of history should be corrected just here. John Wilkes Booth assassinated Lincoln because of no love that he had in his heart for the South, but because Lincoln and Seward had failed to pardon a friend of his, and failing in this promise that friend was hanged. Vengeance was vowed and vengeance was taken. There was not a true man of the South who would have tolerated such a deed as Lincoln's assassination.

What was Lincoln's Reconstruction Policy?

Lincoln's idea was to restore all the seceding States to their rights, extracting a promise that they would not secede again, and that they would free their slaves, because he had promised that in his Proclamation, then punish President Davis and the leaders. He would never have stood for Thad Stevens's policy, and Thad Stevens and his crowd knew it and rejoiced at Lincoln's death.

Now when Southern young men say, "The South as well as the North is ready to admit that Lincoln is the greatest of all Americans," it is full time to call a halt. These young people have been taught to canonize Lincoln, and they must now be taught that Lincoln can never measure up to many of our great men of the South, especially to our Robert E. Lee, a man who in every department of life measured up to the highest standard. Whether as son, husband, father, soldier, teacher, master, citizen, friend, scholar, or Christian gentleman, he presented the most rounded character found in all human history. Lord Wolseley said of him: "He was a being apart and superior to all others in every way; a man with whom none I ever knew, and very few of whom I ever read are worthy to be compared; a man who was cast in a grander mould and made of finer metal than all other men."

Nor am I willing to place Lincoln ahead of our Jefferson Davis. Our Davis never stood for coarse jokes, never violated the Constitution, never stood for retaliation – Lincoln stood for all these. Nor was he even as great as many of the great men of the North. He cannot be compared to our Woodrow Wilson. Many times Lincoln had an opportunity to make peace and he made war. Twice our Woodrow Wilson had an opportunity to plead for peace and he did it. Many times Lincoln had an opportunity to show loving kindness to humanity and many times he failed. Never has there been an opportunity for our President to show loving kindness to those in distress that he has failed.

V.
The Barbara Frietchie Myth

Another wrong that must be righted is the Barbara Frietchie myth. Our children are reciting that poem by Whittier and are being taught that our great and good Stonewall Jackson was not only discourteous but actually revengeful and cruel. We cannot allow this to longer remain unrighted.

I have in my possession a copy of a letter from John G. Whittier written in 1892 in which he acknowledges that he was mistaken in the name of the place where the incident took place and the person mentioned in the poem who waved the flag. He says that a U.S. soldier returning from the war told him the incident, and said that it happened in Maryland when Jackson's troops passed through. He supposed that it took place in Frederick, because Jackson passed through that city, so wrote to the postmaster there to inquire the name of the person connected with the flag waving. The postmaster replied that he had never heard of the incident, but that it sounded very much like Barbara Frietchie, for she was a very patriotic old woman who had lived there at that time. The name struck Whittier as suitable for a poem, so upon that authority only he wrote it.

I have in my possession a copy of a letter from a nephew of Barbara Frietchie, written in 1874 saying that at the time Stonewall Jackson passed through Frederick, Md., he was attending to his aunt's business affairs and he knows positively that she was not able to leave her bed much less to mount a casement to wave a flag.

I have in my possession a copy of a letter from Dr. Zacharias, her pastor, saying that the day before Stonewall Jackson passed through Frederick, he was administering, as to a dying woman, the last communion. He said he knew positively that Barbara Frietchie was not able to go to a window to wave a flag, even had Stonewall Jackson's men passed her home, which they did not.

I have in my possession a chart giving Jackson's line of march in Frederick and the location of Barbara Frietchie's home which was quite off the line. And yet the women of Frederick, knowing these facts, have erected a monument in the streets of that city and lately unveiled it to this falsehood in history.

The U. D. C. Daughters of Frederick protested. The Veterans of the U.C.V. in Frederick protested. The Daughters and Veterans of Maryland protested, and the *Baltimore Sun* protested, but nothing could stop it. The testimony of an old woman over 75 years whose memory is known to be failing has been taken, rather than more reliable testimony. She is a niece of Barbara Frietchie, and has been fed upon this story so long that she really believes it, when her own brother's testimony disproves it. There is nothing to do but to let it be branded in history as a monument to an untruth. The mayor of Frederick was asked why he allowed it to be erected, and he said, "Because it will bring many visitors to our city." Yes, it is a monument unique in history, but does it honor, as a monument should, the memory of anyone? I know Whittier would have resented it, for while we didn't agree with him on the slavery question, he was a man of deep religious convictions and a man who abhorred a sham. If Barbara Frietchie was so patriotic she would not desire an honor that falsified facts.

VI.
Andersonville Prison

Another wrong to be righted and one as much misunderstood by some of our Southern men and women as by those of other sections. I refer to the misrepresentations regarding Andersonville prison, and the unfair trial given to Major Wirz, and the attempt to implicate President Davis in the atrocities, so-called, at Andersonville.

It will be needless to rehearse all the story, especially here in Savannah, for it was a Savannah woman, Mrs. L.G. Young, who wrote the resolutions to introduce in the Georgia Convention U.D.C. when it met in Macon, 1905, to erect a monument to exonerate the name of Wirz and to defend the President of the Confederacy. It was Miss Penning of Columbus, Ga., who seconded it. It was a Savannah woman, Mrs. A.B. Hull, who was President of the Georgia Division when the monument was being erected, although it was unveiled under Miss Alice Baxter's administration. We can bear testimony to endless and vile vituperations hurled at us for daring to defend Major Wirz and the Andersonville atrocities. But we knew that we were right and the truth of history would sustain us; and we knew the attacks came from ignorance of the facts in the case, so we tried to forgive and forget all that was said. We were sorry to stir up strife and bitterness, but right is might and must prevail.

When Senator Blaine in the U.S. Senate Chamber Jan. 10, 1876, cast reproach upon President Davis for the horrors at Andersonville, it was by good Providence that a member of that Senate was Benjamin H. Hill, the confidential adviser of Pres. Davis, and he knew every step that had been taken in the whole affair, and why it was taken. Mr. Hill answered Mr. Blaine.

That was a most remarkable speech. It refuted every accusation brought against Wirz or Davis, and silenced their defamers for a time at least.

I wish I could give Senator Hill's speech in full, but I have not the time or memory to give it, and you have not the time to listen to it. Turning to Mr. Blaine, he said:

> Mr. Blaine, you said Mr Davis was the author knowingly, deliberately, guiltily, and wilfully of the gigantic crime and murder at Andersonville. By what authority do you make this statement? One hundred and sixty witnesses were introduced during the three months trial of Capt. Wirz, and not one mentioned the name of President Davis in connection with a single atrocity. It is true that two hours before Capt. Wirz's execution, parties came to Wirz's confessor saying if "Wirz would

implicate President Davis his sentence would be commuted." What was Wirz's reply? "President Davis had no connection with me as to what happened at Andersonville. Besides, I would not become a traitor even to save my life."

You say, Mr. Blaine, that the food was insufficient and the prisoners were starved to death. The act of the Confederate Congress reads thus: "The rations furnished prisoners of war shall be the same in quantity and quality as those furnished to enlisted men in the army of the Confederacy." That was the law that Mr. Davis approved.

You say, Mr. Blaine, that Mr. Davis sent Gen. Winder to locate a den of horrors. The official order reads thus: "The location for the stockade shall be in a healthy locality, with plenty of pure water, with a running stream, and if possible with shade trees and near to grist and saw mills." This doesn't sound like a den of horrors, does it?

He then rehearsed the efforts of Vice-President Alexander Stephens, Col. Robert Ould, Gen. Howell Cobb, Capt. Wirz, and others, who, time and time again interceded for the exchange of prisoners on any terms and finally on no terms at all, if only they would receive them beyond the borders of the State, and, how every offer was rejected. He showed how medicine, made contraband of war, was denied to be used for their own men. He showed how no act of the Confederate Government was responsible for any horrors that existed at Andersonville, but that all blame must rest wholly with the war policy of the Federal Government. When Gen. Grant was urged to exchange, his answer was, "If we commence a system of exchange we will have to fight until the whole South is exterminated. If we hold those caught they are as dead men."

VII.
Northern Prisons

Mr. Hill continued, "You say, Mr. Blaine, that no prisoners in Northern prisons were ever maltreated. I do not care to unfold the chapters on the other side. I could produce thousands of witnesses from my own State of Georgia alone, to refute this statement."

Yes, Mr. Hill could have told of the horrors of Elmira, Rock Island, Fort Delaware, Camp Chase, and others. And he could have told how the health of Alexander Stephens, our Vice-President, was injured by confinement in Fort Warren, the dampness bringing on an attack of rheumatism from which he never recovered, and which left him a cripple for life. He could have told them how our Sidney Lanier was never a well man after that confinement in a Northern prison. He could have told of those 600 prisoners at Fort Delaware who were placed under the fire of their own men, and guarded by negro soldiers, and he could have told of horrors without end that were heaped upon our prisoners in a spirit of retaliation simply.

Mr. Hill continued:

You say, Mr. Blaine, that President Davis starved and tortured 23,500 prisoners in Southern prisons. Who, Mr. Blaine, starved 26,000 prisoners in Northern prisons? Mr. Stanton, your Secretary of War, gives these statistics, and I feel sure you will believe him, will you not? He says 12% of our men died in your prisons and only 9% of your men died in ours. There were far more Northern men in our prisons than Southern men in your prisons. Why was this per cent. of death greater at the North?

Then turning to Mr. Blaine, Senator Hill said:

No, Mr. Blaine, I tell you this reckless misrepresentations of the South must stop right here. I put you on notice that hereafter when you make an assertion against the South you must be prepared to substantiate full proof thereof.

President Davis sent Gen. Lee under a flag of truce to urge, in the name of humanity, that Gen. Grant agree to an exchange of prisoners. The interview was not granted. This is Gen. Lee's testimony as expressed in a letter to a Philadelphia friend who wished his view of the Andersonville affair: "I offered Gen. Grant to send into his lines all of the prisoners within my Department (Virginia and North Carolina), provided he would return man for man. When I notified the Confederate authorities of my proposition, I was told, if accepted they would gladly place at my disposal every man in our Southern prisons. I also made this offer to the Committee of the U. S. Sanitary Commission – but my propositions were not accepted. – R. E. Lee."

I wish I had time to tell you my conversation with Dr. Kerrof Corsicana, Texas. He was one of our surgeons at Andersonville, and gave me some such valuable history concerning the conditions there. He says to his certain knowledge thirteen of the acts of cruelty brought against Capt. Wirz, and accepted as truth, although absolute proofs were given to the contrary, took place when Capt. Wirz was sick in bed, and some one else in charge of the prisoners. Yes, Wirz was a hero and a martyr.

Dr. Kerr says that Wirz was called hard-hearted and cruel, but he has seen the tears streaming down his face when in the hospitals watching the sufferings of those men. Not a man ever died that he did not see that his grave was distinctly marked so that his mother could come and claim that body. Did anyone at Northern prisons ever do that for our Southern boys' mothers?

If the soldiers hated Wirz, as was said in the trial, why did they not kill him? for they had ample opportunity, as he never went armed. He did not even carry a pocket knife. He once laughingly said to Dr. Kerr that he had an old rusty pistol but it would not shoot.

I have in my library a copy of a set of resolutions which those six paroled prisoners drew up when they returned from Washington, exonerating the Confederate authorities of all blame connected with the horrors of Andersonville prison life, and testifying to the fact that the insults received at Stanton's hands were far harder to bear than anything they ever had suffered at Andersonville.

I have in my library a book written by one of the prisoners exonerating Capt. Wirz and the Confederate authorities. I have in my scrap book a copy of a letter from some of the prisoners sent with a watch which they presented to Capt. Wirz as a token of their appreciation of his kind treatment of them. Mrs. Perrin, his daughter, has many testimonials of this kind.

There was never any trouble about lack of provisions at Andersonville, as has been so often stated. There was an abundant supply of the rations that the soldiers and prisoners needed, but the trouble came because of the over-crowded condition of the stockade. It was made for 10,000 and in four months 29,000 were sent. There were 8,000 sick in the hospitals at one time and no medicines. There were not enough vessels in which the food could be properly prepared and served, and the Confederate authorities were powerless, for they did not have vessels with which to supply this need, nor money with which to buy them.

There were many bad men among the prisoners called "bounty jumpers," and they were killed by their own men, yet Capt. Wirz was accused of their murder. Dr. Kerr said when Capt. Wirz paroled those six prisoners to send them North to plead for exchange, he turned to him and said, "I wish I could parole the last one of them." At the surrender he went to Macon, relying on the honor of Gen. Wilson's parole. Imagine his surprise when he was arrested. He was taken to trial, condemned upon suborned testimony and hanged, Nov. 6, 1865. That was the foulest blot in American history, and Mrs. Surratt's death for complicity with John Wilkes Booth may be placed beside it.

If any one questions the truth of these facts, they can be found verified in the volumes called the *War of the Rebellion*, in the Congressional Library in Washington, D.C, put there by the U.S. authorities.

I have also a copy of a letter from Herman A. Braum of Milwaukee, Wis., who was a prisoner at Andersonville. After paying a tribute to Capt. Wirz and exonerating the Confederate authorities he says, "I believe that there is nothing so well calculated to strengthen the faith in popular government as the example given by the Confederacy during the war, its justice, humanity, and power. On this rests the historic fame of Jefferson Davis."

I wish I had the time to take up some other wrongs and try to right them. I had intended to say something of the Hampton Roads Conference, the Sumner-Brooks caning, and the false history about the *Monitor* and *Merrimac*. But I have detained you too long already, and I must save these for another time.

As I said before, whatever wrongs are righted, they must be righted in the proper spirit.

I know perfectly well what the young people of today will say: "We are tired of hearing of these old issues, don't resurrect them." We have listened to this too long from the young people, and we have allowed them thereby to grow up in ignorance of the truth regarding our history. We must not listen to the many longer. Justice to the living, memory of the dead, a desire that truth may prevail over error and falsehood makes me urgent to right these wrongs of history now.

Our friends from the North do not object to the truth of history provided we are fair and just. We may expect them to disagree with us at times, but that is perfectly natural for they have never heard of many of the things we claim. They, too, have been often wronged in our Southern history aud we must be ready to help them to right their wrongs also. What ever is done, let it be done; in the spirit of truth and peace and love and good will.

It is all right, as President Wilson said, to plan a Lincoln Highway, and it is all right to plan a Jefferson Davis Highway. We should honor the distinguished men of our land. Enough is not done along this line. Foreign countries put ns to shame. Jiut the Lincoln Highway will not obliterate the Mason and Dixon line, as the President suggests, for that is not a line of locality or mere boundary but it is a line of heredity. Just as long as there is pure Puritan blood in the veins of some and pure Cavalier blood in the veins of others, there will be a difference in the thoughts and ways of the people. We cannot be alike if we would. This need not cause a difference that would lead to misunderstandings, however. God grant that never again in the history of our country shall jealousies, bickerings, selfish contentions and political injustice drive us apart. Today we stand, and desire to stand, a reunited people, all sections prosperous, happy, at peace and united. Yes, united in energies, in common interests, in resources, in courage and in patriotism, dependent the one upon the other.

The eyes of the world are on us. There is no doubt that our country is the greatest, the noblest, the mightiest of all the countries of the globe, and we must rejoice at it and keep it so. We should be thankful that we are under a leader who stands for peace and whom the whole world respects, a leader who has come to us "for such a time as this"; a leader who knows no section, but who, knowing the right, dares to maintain it – a leader who has the love of the world in his heart, and would if he could have war to cease and peace and love and harmony prevail throughout the entire world.

Wrongs of History Righted